Collaborating for change?

Managing widening participation in further and higher education

Collaborating for change?

Managing widening participation in further and higher education

Mary Stuart

niace

promoting adult learning

Published by the National Institute of Adult Continuing Education
(England and Wales)
Renaissance House, 20 Princess Road West, Leicester LE1 6TP
Company registration no. 2603322
Charity registration no. 1002775
The NIACE website can be found at www.niace.org.uk

First published 2002
Reprinted 2003
© NIACE

CATALOGUING IN PUBLICATION DATA
A CIP record for this title is available from the British Library
ISBN 1 86201 098 6

Typeset by Q3 Bookwork, Loughborough
Cover design by Boldface
Printed in Great Britain by Antony Rowe, Chippenham, Wiltshire

Contents

1   The magic wand of education – the 'why' and 'how' of widening participation

Widening Participation? It's just a fancy name for what we should be doing. I mean you should be open to everyone (Principal of Northern City College, 1999).

Whether widening participation is a 'fancy name' or not, it is *the big idea* for further and higher education in Britain in the early twenty-first century. Developing and sustaining effective widening participation activities that provide learning for a broader base of society is not as simple as some policy makers had hoped. In a wide-ranging study of adult learning in Britain, Tuckett and Sargant (1999) found that, of the least skilled workers in British society, only a quarter were involved in any form of learning. In examining younger people's participation, Desforges (2000, p 7) notes that:

Something of the order of 10% of 16–19-year-olds 'disappear' from education and work (and hence work-related learning) … Among young people in education and training, drop-out rates on many courses (including NVQ and GNVQ) are unacceptably high. Among those who complete courses at all levels through to first degrees, 'sufficiency' rather than 'excellence' characterises student performance.

The picture painted by this account of learning represents a significant problem in the context of a shifting social order where claims to the development of a knowledge economy are thought to be hindered by the unequal and differentiated participation of young people and adults in ongoing formal learning. Despite a national and, arguably, a global imperative for economic development and the hard work of many practitioners in further and higher education, there is still no evidence that suggests we have been able to find a magic formula to broaden successfully the base of learners to include the most excluded groups in society. It is not as simple as learning a few tips from those who have had some success in widening participation in education. The government targets for widening participation to the post-16 sectors are ambitious (as are many others highlighted in policy documents from the OECD and the EU) and experience suggests a fundamental shift in the perception of the purpose of education needs to occur if such targets are to be met.

The focus for this book is on how to widen participation, how practitioners have managed widening participation in their institution and how they have worked with others to facilitate greater inclusion in education. The book does not try to provide 'final solutions' for the sector but rather, through the case study material examined here, to offer insights that can move the debates and practice of widening participation forward.

The book specifically focuses on further education colleges and universities. I have not dealt with the many other smaller providers such as voluntary or public sector adult education or higher education (HE) colleges. Innovation is a feature of many smaller institutions and certainly widening participation has been a major strand of adult education provision since its development in the nineteenth century. But, as Field (2000, p 41) points out, 'by the mid-1980s, the further education colleges had overtaken local authority adult education centres as providers of education and training for adults.' Further education (FE) colleges and universities are being expected to develop new ways of working and are being expected to work with a broader base of learners than ever before.

Although influenced by theory, the book is rooted in practice. The thinking behind the book developed out of nearly 20 years of my own practice, as a teacher, development worker and manager in adult, F and HE. All of my work in this field has, in one form or another, been concerned with developing educational equality and the research for the book developed from discussions with a range of people involved in widening participation who provide what I would call 'good enough practice'. In other words, I am not talking about idealised solutions but practice that grows out of real environments and is made to work in complex situations.

I have written the book in the first person and do not obscure my own position on issues, nor do I exclude my own background in the field, which has led me to research and write the book. For me, it is vital that we are honest about our own starting point because it enables you, the reader, to position me, the author and my work, within a social framework. I do not believe it is possible to make wholly objective judgements. Knowledge is developed within the social realm, within communities and is contextual. All our values are related to our relative positions (Duncan, 1996) within society and it is this positioning of myself and the book that I detail in the next section.

Positions and perspectives – life experience and widening participation

Most of the people who work in the field of educational equality have had to reinvent themselves on a regular basis, depending on the current policy and funding language. For many, their lived experience provides evidence that some of the core principles of widening participation are not new but have simply altered over time. My career, and those of many of my colleagues, began in unpaid volunteering, sometimes gaining small grants to develop new learning opportunities in a local area, some within formal education settings and some elsewhere. As another experienced, community development worker put it:

> The problem with all these things is the sort of funding regimes that underpin the work. We constantly fall over the same people at meetings because we feel like we daren't miss an opportunity for funding, in case it means the difference between survival or not (Coare, 2000, p 32).

During the 1980s and 1990s much of this work in further and higher education was for adult learners providing a range of return-to-study possibilities. When the Universities Funding Council announced special funding for work with the 'educationally disadvantaged' in the early 1990s, many access and guidance practitioners moved from further/adult education or the youth service into higher education. We found our position, as marginal members of marginal departments in universities, as comfortable as any before. Other colleagues remained in FE, often battling against an increasingly corporatist management culture (Zera and Jupp, 1998). The publication of *The Learning Age* (DfEE, 1997) drew widening participation in F and HE from the margins into the mainstream. This process meant that the focus and nature of practitioners' work shifted once more. Working with young people became an increasing feature of what had, until then, been largely focused on adult learning (Layer, 2001a). This shift towards working with young people, even working with schools, has been significant and remains something that practitioners still struggle to address. In a climate of dissolving boundaries, the outcomes expected of widening participation in F and HE are diverse and practice, no matter our previous experience, needs to take account of this need for greater diversity. It seems important that before we examine the 'how' of widening participation, we should ask some 'why' questions, such as: 'Why widen participation in post-16 education in the first place?'; 'Why is partnership and collaboration thought to be the way to do so?'; and, finally, 'Why produce a book on *managing* that process?'. The rest of this chapter focuses on these 'why' questions.

Why widening participation?

Much of the current rhetoric growing out of widening participation initiatives is rooted in a naive vision of education as a magic wand that can solve the growing gap between the knowledge 'haves' and the learning 'have nots'. As Edwards and Miller (2000, p 17) point out:

> Positioning education as the root of exclusion or maybe even as the route to inclusion suggests a simplified causal relationship that might make sense to education ministers trying to secure resources from treasuries, but excludes possible alternative analyses of the situation.

Certainly, education can make a difference to people's lives but it is not a panacea for all social ills and does not necessarily lead to greater opportunities for different groups to participate more equally in society. As Field (2000, p 126) points out in relation to government-run programmes to combat unemployment: 'State-managed programmes are often ill suited to the flexibility and adaptability of a post-Fordist labour market … Evidence suggests that conventional supply-side strategies on their own have a limited impact upon inclusion.'

Equally, while the sentiment of an education open to all seems just, over-zealous missionaries of widening participation often do not see the increasing levels of coercion in our education and training discourses. Such programmes often *require* unemployed people to learn, a form of compulsion which, argu-ably, could have been thought to fail with the same people during their pre-16 education.

Some people have argued that widening participation creates lowered stan-dards, the old 'dumbing down' chestnut. Equally, some practitioners in both F and HE are concerned that the economic benefits of learning which are now well researched (Bynner and Egerton, 2001) may be reduced if participation rates increase substantially as the value of qualifications may reduce as more learners attain accreditation (Morgan, 2001). Widening participation itself is not a concept where there is consensus and, while I discuss in more detail different perspectives on widening participation in Chapter 2, it is important to point out here that the argument for widening participation in learning has to be based on a range of social and personal benefits and needs. Clearly, there is no intrinsic value to any qualification and increasingly better-paid employment requires higher level qualifications. However, learning is not only about gaining recogni-tion and creating better earning power, the so-called 'education dividend'. It is also about self-fulfilment and an ability to gain access to understanding that enables people to be more active and powerful citizens. The education system was born out of a battle between those who believed in learning equality and those who wanted to create a series of exclusive learning systems designed to provide an appropriate workforce required for nineteenth-century industrialisa-tion. At the heart of the current widening participation agenda is a similar set of battles in a new economic era. It is the continuation of this older battle that concerns many practitioners, especially those who come from the adult educa-tion and access movement. I discuss some of the prior struggles in greater detail in Chapter 2, and take up the question of the changing social and economic order in more detail in Chapter 8.

As society changes and our global order is re-aligned, the imperative for people to learn only grows. Knowledge development in a society is not like a cake, where once each part is apportioned it is simply used up. Rather knowledge is like a spiral: as more is learned so there is a need for new knowledge. There is therefore no question about the need for ongoing learning, but questions do remain about who has access to that learning. Currently, in Britain at least, widening participa-tion has a specific focus on redressing the class-based elitism that has dominated our educational institutions since their inception. In other words, during the nine-teenth and twentieth centuries, higher-level learning was dominated by the middle classes and much of further education was designed for the so-called 'artisan class'. In a more equitable society, there would be a more even distribution of learners from different social backgrounds and with different experience. Hence, widening participation is not just about increasing the numbers of people learning but also about greater diversity of learners. Achieving that greater diversity, while not creating a magic wand for a 'better' society, should provide greater opportunity for development across the whole of society. If we accept that not only do we have to increase the numbers of people learning beyond compulsory education levels to develop our society for the new economy, but also to ensure that we have equal access to such learning for all groups in society, then we need to examine the means to achieve that. Currently the rhetoric in Britain is that access can only be achieved by working together with other agencies. The next section examines why collaboration is seen as the way forward.

Why collaboration?

As well as current policy, which encourages activities towards inclusion, lifelong learning and participation, education practitioners are also currently encouraged to work in 'partnership' or collaborate with other providers. In Britain, over the past five years, a plethora of partnerships has emerged that encourage collaboration as a means to develop more effective provision. To name just a few: local learning partnerships, widening participation project partnerships, regeneration partnerships and learning city partnerships. One could perhaps be forgiven for wondering if all this so-called 'joined-up thinking' is limiting the opportunity for real work, when being involved in so many different partnerships takes up so much time and energy.

The definition of collaboration has changed somewhat over the past 50 years. Working with others, or joint approaches to solutions, seems a more appropriate way of expressing the model of practice being discussed here, but sometimes the working together feels like working with the enemy as the term collaboration can imply. Working closely with people from different organisations with different cultures is not as simple as some policy makers have envisaged. As one of the interviewees for this book pointed out when I asked him about partnerships:

> I think there is too much hype about it. We're all encouraged to collaborate, the word collaborate has changed a bit ... when you think about in the middle of the last century where collaborators were not welcome. The language is fascinating. We were supposed to compete during the 1980s and now we're supposed to collaborate ... I believe very, very strongly that tremendous value can be gained from really working in partnership, but a lot of partnerships around are shotgun partnerships and when you've got a shotgun partnership, it doesn't work (Director of Continuing Education, Northern University, 2000).

Partnership working is not always the best solution to developing practice and before partnerships are developed, potential partners should examine if there is 'added value' to working together (Action on Access, 2001). The development of partnerships as one solution to the difficulties of participation is discussed in more detail in Chapter 4, along with examples of, and approaches to, partnership working. However here it is important to point out that increasingly we are aware that learning cannot be seen in isolation from other areas of people's lives. If this is the case, working with others in different fields of social development and from other areas of the education sector will form an important support mechanism for expanding and widening participation in F and HE.

Collaboration and partnership between groups and individuals has the potential to transform education, shifting from its current modernist discourse to a more relevant approach to learning for the 21st century. I do not have a magic wand, but some of the approaches recounted in this book inspired me to believe there are ways that we can create an education that is both challenging and exciting for the many people who currently do not engage in formal education beyond an age when they can escape from it. Many people who have been involved in widening participation activities over the years will be suspicious of any book that focuses on management. Is management about elitism, about those that have a say in running things excluding those who actually know about doing things – or is this approach necessarily the only way to manage? The next section sets out the position adopted in this book for managing widening participation and collaborative ventures.

Why manage the process? – Questions of margins and centres

The book is aimed at anyone who is involved in widening participation activities in F and HE. It takes a broad view of management, recognising that managing is not only about strategy, resources and supporting people but also about managing activity. I hope to provide some clues for new managers who are coming into the sector on how to work within what we currently term post-16 education. I also hope that the book provides, in some modest way, new ideas for development and innovation within and beyond institutions for more established colleagues involved in managing widening participation in the F and HE sectors.

Many of the people who are involved in widening participation activities in universities and colleges have had different career paths to conventional academics. Widening participation specialists often find they are expected to change practice in their institutions without being given any training in how the structures and systems of their new organisations operate. One of my interviewees, a middle manager in a new university, put it this way:

> I found it difficult at first … no one told me that universities were anarchic organisations or where they emerged [from] and how their values had been derived … It can be very imposing. You have got to develop an understanding of the organisation and how it works.
>
> I talk to people a lot about how do we find people who do grass-roots stuff who have a strategic sense. It is a lot to ask of people. Seldom do you have an idea of strategy unless you have been in a management role. You have not had that experience and it is hard (Access and Guidance Co-ordinator, 1999).

Most people who have engaged in widening participation activities consider themselves to be 'outsiders' to the mainstream of education. Of course, precisely how marginal we are is debatable when we have secure jobs in the education sector. Marginality is itself an interesting concept when talking about inclusion and it is perhaps ironic that many people who like to work on the fringe of their institution are especially concerned to 'include' other marginal groups in the mainstream of society. The idea of marginality and its role in developing change is discussed further in Chapter 3.

Many who have been 'marginal' remain on the fringes of their institutions, often not connected with activities elsewhere. However, as the National Task-force for Widening Participation pointed out, learning from such marginal experience is crucial. They say (2000, p 90) that it is important to 'build in time to find out what is going on nationally and regionally for similar groups of students. That way you benchmark the effectiveness of your activities and can pick up on some other alternative approaches'. Valuing marginality is something that managers in the sector need to consider more seriously because innovation is often developed in such spaces where there is an interface between an organisation and the rest of society.

For many, partly because of their marginal position, the concept of management itself seems alien and slightly suspect. I, as have many others, have had to accept the fact that as my working life has developed I am no longer directly involved in what we term 'outreach' but far more involved in management. This book is an attempt to face up to that reality and examine the concept of management in an area of education, equality work, that has consistently offered challenges to the status quo and to established practices. The book is not about being a 'boss', someone who has patriarchal (or matriarchal!) authority to hire and fire staff and dictate an organisation's direction. It concerns management as a process of development in which all participants share responsibility. Managing is not an individual responsibility but a process of working with others. In other words, it is about collaboration or partnership between different people within and beyond individual organisations. This is perhaps a more radical approach to engaging people in development and innovation. These ideas are discussed further in Chapters 3 and 4. To conclude this chapter, I discuss how the book developed over a period of several years.

Gathering material – a note about methodology

The material in the book grew out of a series of case studies. At its broadest level, the research was drawn from the experience of managers in F and HE in England. Although specific to a particular policy context, this case study does provide an example of global transformations in education in late/post modernity. At a more detailed level, the research is based on interviews with individual managers in F and HE. It is their reflections on, and observations of, their practice in managing change in their institutions that have informed the examples in this book. Work of this nature can provide us with realistic accounts of experience and can offer a useful way of interrogating what we do:

> Exploratory studies of this kind can serve to place question marks over commonly held views, and to throw up suggestions and hypotheses as a basis for further work (Searle-Chatterjee, 1999, p 261).

I began the research for this book in 1999 and completed the interviews in 2000. I had become increasingly concerned that a divide between managers in the F and HE sectors and those who work 'on the ground', in communities and with students, was becoming even more distinct than previously. As I became more involved in management, I found that most of the literature in the field did not address my needs. It seemed that management within F and HE had largely been articulated within the context of managing budgets, student numbers, quality management, measurable outcomes and human resource concerns. As a recent addition of *College Research* highlighted:

> The emphasis [has been] on funding, management, markets and growth. Now interest is reviving in ... the policy priorities of widening participation, raising achievement and extending social inclusion (Morris, 2000, p 4).

Work in communities, or aspiration-raising with young people, requires a different set of knowledges, with much of the work being difficult to quantify and therefore to justify from simple targets. Widening participation therefore offers a challenge to managers to reformulate their practice and re-conceive their role in strategic planning. Equally, tutors and community development educationalists need to rethink their approach to management.

I wanted to find examples from the field that could help me develop my own practice. I chose a range of managers from different institutions located in contrasting settings: three FE college managers, two old-university managers and three new-university managers from across England. Because of different approaches to education in Scotland and Wales, the case studies in the book have only been drawn from England but many of the ideas are transferable to other contexts. The interviewees were chosen for different reasons; their experience of widening participation work, their involvement in strategic or tactical management, the institution where they worked, their gender, ethnicity and their commitment to a vision of a more equitable education system. Some of my interviewees have been colleagues or managers in institutions where I have worked, others I knew through national widening participation networks and some of those interviewed I only knew from their reputation in the field. I could have chosen others, several of whom I know to be excellent practitioners. I would not want to suggest that the people discussed in this book are necessarily the 'best' managers in the field but together they represent a diverse and interesting group of individuals who do, I think, critically reflect on current educational policy and practice in the sector.

A common thread that draws all of my interviewees together is their perception of themselves as 'yes people'. One of my interviewees, a middle manager at a new university, put it this way:

> I can't say no, so I get loaded up with loads of work and I forget I have 101 things on my plate. It is something I wish I could change because sometimes it pulls me away from things that I should be giving more time to (Director of Continuing Education, Central University, 1999).

However, he also saw it as a positive way of enabling development:

> You get a very broad perspective on things, as you are involved in all kinds of developments. People on the outside may say 'how does that relate to what you were doing yesterday?' but you can see it. I think it does have a connection; it is not always very clear but more often than not, it is appropriate. It is a very higgledy-piggledy process to management but it does produce creative solutions sometimes.

The majority of the case study material is contained in Chapter 5, which provides institutional case studies from further education; Chapter 6, which discusses universities; and Chapter 7, which focuses on the role of individuals in developing change.

The interviewees were also involved in different types and levels of management within their institutions, but the issues that they raise are reflected in much of the literature and policy documents from across the world. While there are some specificities within each situation, there are also general points which I hope will have echoes for readers in very different environments. I have not used the actual names of my interviewees but have focused on their position within their institution. I have also used pseudonyms for their institution. Each pseudonym is based on the geographical location of the college or university concerned. Nevertheless, while respecting their privacy, I have attempted to give voice to my interviewees and have wherever possible used their actual words rather than my interpretation of them. It seemed important that they were able to 'speak for themselves' and while I have developed models for their practice and, therefore, categorised their management style, I have tried to ensure that the book reflects the different voices that I heard. I hope in this way that something of their different personalities becomes visible.

Widening participation for a changing society?

Britain's tertiary education system is very diverse. There are not only different sets of funding arrangements between further and higher education, but also within each funding regime, there are other dividers. There are not only FE colleges, but also sixth form colleges, community colleges and voluntary sector providers of adult education who are all funded by the Learning and Skills Council. Within HE, there continues, despite nearly ten years of living with one funding body for England, a divide between what are termed 'old' and 'new' universities. There are also divides within the 'old' university sector with some of this group seen to be more elitist with a large student base, the so-called Russell Group while smaller 'old' universities have united under the banner of the 1994 Group. Equally 'further' and 'higher' learning is not necessarily any longer confined to institutions displaying those titles. Changing growth patterns show that while numbers grew in HE substantially between 1988 and 1994, in the past five years there has been more growth within FE colleges. Much of the prized research in science has developed outside the academy in the commercial world. The nature of society across the world is changing. Whether we call this post-modernism or late modernity or late capitalism is perhaps not that important; the fact is that the way we are organising our lives is very different from 50 years ago. Usher *et al* (1997, p 2) put it this way:

> With this contemporary form of capital accumulation has come post-Fordist forms of work organisation and management – flatter management structures, team-work, quality assurance procedures, a decline in centralised trade union bargaining power and ... a demand for a multi-skilled work-force.

There is considerable talk about the knowledge economy and the information society. At the heart of these sound bites is an expression of a profound change. Lyotard (1984) argues that knowledge is being replaced by information that can be assimilated through information technologies. In other words, knowledge has become commodified. Communications between people are much faster and access to information is no longer solely the preserve of the 'expert' (Giddens, 1990). 'The boundaries of the nation state have been breached by globalizing trends in the economy, communications, migration, tourism, etc ... The notion of society, therefore, has come to be seen as problematic ...' (Edwards, 2000, p 9). This has significant implications for our education systems, not only post-16 education, of course, but all education. Hence, when looking at the 'field' of education, the picture is confusing for any outsider and there remains the suggestion that the boundaries between institutions, communities, learning and learners are being eroded. The final chapter explores trends for the futures of F and HE in the 21st century.

For some, the current climate threatens all that education has stood for, while for others it is an opportunity to develop education as it should be and at the heart of this debate is the term 'widening participation'. The rest of the book examines these issues highlighted in this first chapter and offers different approaches to the process of widening engagement with further- and higher-level study.

2 Slippery notions and powerful potions – perspectives on widening participation in further and higher education

Widening participation is the current catch-all phrase that encompasses a range of activities and ideas, many of which have had long histories in the debates about the purpose of education itself. For most educationalists, widening participation is linked to notions of educational equality, but over time the question of who is being targeted in this 'widening' process in further and higher education has changed. Initially, debates focused on what is now compulsory education. During the nineteenth century battles about access to learning focused on basics like literacy for working class children and their parents. What began as a struggle for rights and entitlements for young people has become, in current education practice, a compulsion to obtain a limited set of standards in pre-16 education (Field, 2000).

At the beginning of the 20th century, increasing the participation of women, particularly middle-class women, in HE was a significant campaign. Running alongside these different battles for educational equality was a concurrent set of economic imperatives. Modernity increasingly required a literate and reliable workforce trained to support and sustain a diverse economy. Campaigns for equality and access to education for all in society were more attractive to policy makers and governments when it was clear that the needs of the economy could also be served by increasing participation. With its diverse historical roots, widening participation is understandably a concept that is often relatively intangible and enjoys several different meanings. Currently, widening participation is linked to concern about retention as well as access because there is a recognition that it is not enough to bring people into an education system but that they also must be able to progress through it.

The current debate about widening participation in F and HE has echoes of the dichotomy between economic need and social justice campaigns of the 19th and 20th centuries, and its meaning should not be taken for granted in practice. In this chapter, I examine the different meanings of widening participation in the context of F and HE in Britain today. I discuss how different interpretations of widening participation have affected day-to-day practice, and examine how the current emphasis on collaborative approaches to widening participation presents challenges for the sector.

The concern about participation is not only a British problem but is also a global phenomenon and the chapter explores some of the continuities in discourse across different countries. The past few years have seen considerable rhetoric about change in education and this chapter highlights some of the issues that arise from the plethora of policy documents and government legislation that have sharpened the debate since 1996. It also argues that the changes that have taken, and are taking, place in F and HE are not happening in a vacuum but are being built on prior practice within the sector. For, as Pritchard (2000, p 46) points out in his evaluation of management practices in F and HE:

> The years 1997–2000 may in retrospect mark the beginning of a major re-construction of FE colleges and universities in the UK ... Resistance to the Blairite expectation that colleges and universities will co-operate and form partnerships seems inevitable following years of direct competition for students and funding between decentralised, corporately-focused colleges and universities. The managerial station in colleges and universities is ... largely an effect of the Thatcherite power bloc. Current and future reconstruction will be mediated against this formulation.

In other words, any evaluation of a more collaborative approach to widening participation needs to be understood in the context of earlier debates, which emphasise the 'product' elements of education, where learning is provided in neatly packaged bite- (or byte-) sized chunks, competitively priced and cleverly marketed. In her review of FE, Kennedy (1997, p 3) found an extensive climate of competition:

> Competition has been interpreted by some colleges as a spur to go it alone. Other colleges are seen as rivals for students rather than as potential collaborators with whom good practice and a strategic overview can be shared and developed.

This 'customer' focused corporate approach to learning is still evident in much F and HE practice, not only in Britain but also in the rest of Europe and in the United States. The chapter begins with a discussion on the roots of the current concerns about participation.

Widening participation, targeting and massification

Education providers are not isolated or simply autonomous. Rather, they work within a broader context of more general social policies, where their direction is shaped by politicians and funders who are themselves influenced by policy strat-egists and electoral demands. In other words, education has always been particularly political, and the participation debate, which grew to dominate policy during the 1970s and beyond, was a political debate about the targeting of limited resources as well as the particular needs of groups of learners. Despite the ideal of education for all,[1] finally enshrined in the 1944 Education Act in

Britain, the social transformation in achievement that was expected had not been realised by the 1970s and increasingly budgets, especially for non-statutory provision, were under strain. To take adult learning as an example, although it grew enormously between 1961 and 1975 in all its different forms, as Stock (1996) notes, students tended to come from middle-class backgrounds, usually as recurrent learners. In higher education, the Robbins Report (1963) reframed the definition of HE and suggested alternative methods of funding in the sector. The development of the polytechnics from the recommendations of Robbins heralded the beginning of a mass HE system. It challenged the 'classical' curriculum of HE and increased the numbers of individual participants in the HE system.

However, while this development increased the numbers of students going into HE, there continued to be a substantial number of what came to be termed non-participants in any form of post-16 education. Robbins based his report on a participation rate of just six per cent of the population (Layer, 2001b, p 10). The polytechnic sector worked to attract students who came from more diverse backgrounds into their vocationally-orientated programmes. The older universities continued to provide extra-mural programmes, largely with an increasingly middle-class student group. Stock (1996) argues that with the reduction in resources for adult education during the 1970s targeting specific groups who were non-participants became popular, heralding the expansion and development of Adult Basic Education (ABE) and English for Speakers of Other Languages (ESOL). 'We may be certain that there was a sea change in the perception of both central and local government as to what constituted 'useful' education for adults and for most this meant basic education' (Stock, 1996, p 17).

In FE, the role of basic education became a significant feature of budgets. Non-learners, especially those who had not succeeded within initial education, became the target of government funding and institutional mission. In response, a barrage of interventionist-style policies and programmes were introduced, including the famous literacy campaign of the 1970s and equal-opportunities-directed funds from local authorities such as the Inner London Education Authority (ILEA) in the early 1980s.

Within further and adult education institutions, a range of different strategies was adopted. Adult Basic Education took very different forms in different parts of the country. For some, the work of Freire (1972) gave an emancipatory vision to their work, including developing the oral history of working class and refugee peoples and developing a feminist consciousness-raising programme for women. On the other hand the government emphasis during the 1980s shifted towards a greater concern for economic development and the needs of the workforce. The connection was drawn between unemployment and basic skills: 'In 1991, the government emphasised the key role of the colleges in an "education and training strategy" and committed the government to encouraging growth in this area' (Gallacher and Thomson, 1999, p 14).

Gallacher and Thomson go on to point out that this move towards highlighting the skill development imperative of FE began to encompass HE as well. They say:

[a] growing emphasis on widening access to further and higher education ... emerged in the second half of the 1980s. This was also associated with the economic arguments insofar as the government was keen to tap education and training in society, and this resulted in a growing interest in attracting more adult students to return to education with a view to improving their qualifications and skills (Gallacher and Thomson, 1999, p 14).

Access programmes also developed during the 1980s and validating bodies sprang up all over the country. FE colleges dominated the Access market. It was largely women, who had been denied education earlier in their lives, who drew down that entitlement, perhaps because of the feminist influence in adult basic education and in other adult and further education programmes. In the twenty-first century, the gender balance in HE has shifted to a situation where more than half of undergraduates are now women but the terms of their participation in HE still create cause for concern (Thompson, 1995).

In the early 1990s, the funding council for universities developed a similar approach to that employed by local authorities during the 1980s. With a reducing unit of resource, specific funding was allocated for work with 'educationally disadvantaged groups'. In other words, a shift in thinking had occurred about the role of higher education, which had been dominated by a focus on a particular sort of higher-level curriculum to a concern with the participation of such groups as the 'socially alienated'. Like local authority provision that had assumed during the 1960s that increasing provision itself would increase the participation rates of 'alienated' groups, universities were increasingly ending up teaching middle-class students rather than working-class people. Like local authorities, intervention and the targeting of specific groups became the strategy and policy of funders and government.

The language of the 'educationally disadvantaged' was, of course, based on a deficit model. In attempts to secure funds, whether in universities or FE colleges, staff increasingly had to define their communities as deficient. Targeting specific groups, therefore, who are not participating (McGivney, 1992) seldom implied that the system had to change; rather the implication was that the targeted groups had to change. During this period, caps on funded numbers in the sector were removed – although the unit of resource was reducing.

During the 1990s FE colleges, through the 1992 Further and Higher Education Act (F and HE Act), were encouraged to develop corporate identities, taking on many of the trappings of commercial business. The rationale for this practice was that if FE was to develop a skilled workforce, they needed to understand the needs of business. More fundamentally, government was determined to attract a more diverse funding base for colleges, especially private funding, to reduce the sector's dependence on state funding. Additionally, competition between colleges over even more limited resources became the most significant distinguishing factor of the sector between 1992 and 1998. Colleges were encouraged to compete to increase their numbers. Successful colleges could gain additional funding for specific types of students taking accredited programmes. Pritchard

(2000, p 29) eloquently points out the impact of this development on the staff in institutions:

> Workers in further/higher education are involved in a fundamental reconstruction of the sector from public service to public enterprise. Attempts are being made to intensify the effectiveness of labour, to reduce costs and increase non-state income. Yet this is not simply a mechanical programme that can be read off from the prescriptions found in the managerial texts or from one set of college or university management financial statements ... it involves the reconstruction of identities.

The F and HE Act also affected higher education by allowing polytechnics to take on university status. By ending the divide between polytechnics and universities, government aimed to increase competition and 'consumer choice' in HE.

In 1995, new funds for 'widening provision' were made available to all universities, old and new, through competitive bidding. Widening provision could be a challenging term. It is not about participation, but examining and changing provision within the academy. In other words, this tranche of monies suggested a different perspective to that of previous targeting. Implicit in this funding was a belief that 'targeted groups', the non-participants in HE, required guidance in order to facilitate their move into and through the system. It was based on numerous reports and articles (Fraser, 1999; Houghton, 1998; Johnston and Croft, 1998; NIACE, 1993) that access required information, and retention required guidance. Successful applications for funds used guidance as a major plank of their strategic plans for the use of these funds. However, while the notion of guidance about routes into and through HE was less patronising than the language incorporating the idea of the 'educationally disadvantaged', it was still focused on a taken-for-granted structure of HE learning, highlighting student retention, successful completion, credits and qualifications.

FE was also encouraged to provide guidance for students; in fact formula funding required provision for guidance, as well as developing packages of support for different students. Using the funding mechanism, specific types of courses were privileged, usually those with a vocational outcome that were accredited. This shaped the nature of FE and changed the provision offered significantly. Colleges retrenched into main buildings, moving out of community settings where they felt unable to provide the range of support provision now required. They moved away from courses that did not lead to qualifications. They also looked increasingly to what was considered to be higher-status work, such as HE courses within their colleges, which grew considerably during the 1990s, suggesting that the distinction between F and HE institutions was becoming less marked (Gallacher and Thomson, 1999, p 16). Hence, the 1992 Act was designed to:

> introduce market principles to education, and to give 'customers' a more central role in influencing the type of programmes provided within the colleges. This led to the removal of colleges from local authority control, and establish them as free-standing corporate bodies with their own

budgets and employing their own staff (Gallacher and Thomson, 1999, p 14).

Joint ventures between F and HE were already in place. Alliances between Higher Education Institutions (HEIs) and FE colleges were seen as a way for both parties to grow, as Schuller *et al* (1999, p 28) pointed out:

> The present pattern of further–higher education links arose during the period of rapid expansion in full-time higher education; the capping of student numbers, together with the consequences of incorporation and other developments in higher education, create a new context.

Massification was taking hold. By this time, numbers of participants in HE had risen from less than one in five of the population in the 1960s to one in three in the 1990s. However, the numbers of people from poorer backgrounds participating in HE had decreased (Wicks, 2000). Perceptions of participation in learning in the EU also began to highlight this discrepancy (Delors, 1996).

The range of policy strategies and legislation from the second half of the 20th century (F and HE Act, 1992; Robbins, 1963) attempted to widen access but had not managed to, despite claims that massification and a HE system based on continuing learning were being established (Duke, 1992). Neither FE nor HE had succeeded in attracting the broad-based student population expected. More recent widening participation strategies are, therefore, rooted in a sense that change was necessary to attract new students from the poorest communities in Britain (Fryer, 1997). As Kennedy (1997, p 5) points out:

> There has been growth but the students recruited have not come from a sufficiently wide cross-section of the community and there is concern that initiatives to include more working class people, more disaffected young people, more women, more people from ethnic minority groups are being discontinued because they fall through the gaps in the system ... Even with the exciting expansion of further and higher education, the children of the working class have not been the real beneficiaries.

This is particularly highlighted by Sargant *et al* (1997, vi):

> Social class continues to be the key discriminator in understanding participation in learning. Over half of all upper and middle-class (AB) respondents are current or recent learners, compared with one-third of the skilled working class (C2) and one-quarter of unskilled working people and people on limited incomes (DE).

However, although these statistics seem stark indicators of the failure of education to attract a broad-based clientele for learning, the measures used to identify learning are contested. For example, Tight has sounded a note of caution in the measurement of participation in learning. He suggests (Tight, 1998, p 117) that Sargant's work:

> rests on the belief that most adults are non-participants in lifelong learning. As such, they are seen as a problem, and must be persuaded to become regular and enthusiastic participants. The politics of participation do not

seem to be concerned, therefore, except at a general and rhetorical level, with lifelong learning in its broad and all-encompassing sense ... Rather lifelong learning is being interpreted in a narrower and more limited way, both in government policy statements and in the national reports that inform them.

Similarly, in a global context Tobias (1998, p 134) has suggested that:

> People's patterns of learning and education can be understood only in the context of their life-worlds. It is a distortion of reality to see participation as a dichotomous event, and it is even more of a distortion to equate non-participation with non-learning.

The focus on participation in formal learning suggests a greater interest in the needs of the economy rather than learning that individuals and groups wish to develop for their own interest. Others in the field have also questioned that the 'working class' can be seen as an entity in itself. Westwood points out that our perceptions of the working class are based in a false notion of community, as if it is a homogeneous group. Rather she suggests that the working class is fractured. She says: 'The working class has never been a single unitary subject but has been simultaneously fractured by skill, gender, ethnicity, region and the cultures engendered by these divisions' (1992, p 234).

The contradictions and fractures created by categorisations such as gender, ethnicity dis/ability and age were not identified as a central part of the working class 'communities' targeted for participation in F and HE. Thus community was located within a consensus constructed around 'the hegemony of white Englishness and homogenised as the "community" becoming itself the subject/object of educational intervention' (Usher *et al*, 1997, p 39). The picture of participation is more complex, more slippery to grasp, especially in a target/outcome-driven environment. Yet it is this climate in which managers in F and HE find themselves, and it is to this climate that they must respond.

In the next section, I argue that despite significant changes in government policy since 1997, simplistic outcome-driven measures have still been enforced although the ideology behind the new participation strategy is more 'welfarist' than the simple market-based approach of the previous 20 years.

Widening participation as inclusion

The overall thrust of the Labour government's arguments for widening participation focuses on an education for inclusion across society not just in learning, but also inclusion in the workplace, in civic society and in the community. Like the government before them, a major part of the agenda for widening participation in F and HE is expressed in terms of the needs of global capitalism where 'upskilling' is the main focus of learning 'taken up over the lifespan' (Wicks, 2000). On this side of the debate, standards are equated with benchmarking, providing 'what students and employers can expect from a course' (Wicks, 2000). The placing of employers as equal 'stakeholders' to students is of course not just a British phenomenon. Tobias (1998, p 15) points out that: 'Almost all countries face changes in employment structures and the subsequent issue of the relevance of education to a changing world of work, particularly secondary and higher education.'

International competitiveness developed through a new education agenda is a central underlying principle for many of the changes that have occurred in Britain since 1997. At the heart of the government's rationale for the development of FE and redefining the purpose of HE is the need for competitiveness in the market place. This approach to learning can be found across most of the developed world, as Gallacher and Thomson (1999, p 15) lucidly explain:

> [these developments] can all be seen as part of a growing emphasis on establishing a 'learning society' and establishing conditions, to promote lifelong learning which the current government has emphasised in its educational policy (DfEE 1998; Fryer, 1997; DfEE, 1999a). This can be seen as part of a wider agenda which has been emerging in many countries throughout Europe and indeed other parts of the world.

Equally, they point out (1999, p 15), there is, unlike in previous approaches, an emphasis on developing society and social responsibility:

> in many of these documents there is also an emphasis on the vital role which education can have as a contributor to creating greater social cohesion and in tackling problems of social exclusion (Kennedy, 1997; Fryer, 1997).

In Britain, the central plank in the government's strategy to tackle social exclusion was the establishment of the Social Exclusion Unit. The Unit's work is premised on a belief that the public services that were designed to create social and economic wealth and well-being needed to work together to produce results. The Kennedy Report (1997) took an approach that highlighted such forms of intervention. She suggested (1997, p 33) that: 'Collaborative interagency approaches should be adopted locally ... The divisions that exist are sometimes made worse by the way they are managed.'

Kennedy was pointing out that previous attempts to include 'hard-to-reach' students had been mishandled. Many of these failings can be attributed to an inability to move beyond the competing needs of individual institutions. Given the context in which such 'partnerships' were born, managers in the sector have felt unable to work with others because they are competing for funds, competing for students and concerned to achieve performance indicators that will be measured against their so-called partner's performance.

Another important element of recent developments in widening participation has been the re-invention of local and regional strategy. Kennedy (1997, 39) talked about the waste of resource put into unproductive meetings:

> Many of the key local stakeholders in post-16 education and training therefore meet repeatedly in different forums to discuss similar and linked issues. We are concerned that this flowering of consultation, partnership and inter-agency networking is often focused on single issue activities and masks the absence of any fully effective local strategic dimension in determining the character of and priorities for public investment in FE. The

absence of a strategic dimension at local level is, in our view, a major weakness in the system which significantly reduces the potential for widening participation.

In other words, it has been recognised that working together is more complex than just meeting together. She went on to recommend the development of local partnerships that had an overview of strategy. Two different attempts have been made to address this recommendation, particularly for the further education sector: learning partnerships and the development of regional bases for the Learning and Skills Council (LSC). The LSC was established to draw together work in 'further education, workbased training and young people workforce development, adult and community learning, information, advice and guidance for adult and education business links' (Learning and Skills Council, 2001) but not higher education. The council is centrally located but operates locally through 47 offices. The move from a funding body in the further education funding council to a more regionally-focused planning body like the LSC is significant and highlights the Labour government's determination to be more interventionist in individual college management. In its draft corporate plan, the LSC indicates that regional planning will be developed. The Council recognises that the national training targets have not taken account of local need and it is their explicit intention to ensure that future practice changes this:

> We intend by March 2002 that each local council will have developed a local strategic plan ... Each plan will contribute towards national needs, but will also ensure that education and training provision fully meets local economic and social needs (Learning and Skills Council, 2001, p 11).

While these developments perhaps provide a clearer process for developing strategy, they have not addressed the disjuncture between F and HE which often remains outside the remit of these regional or local partnerships, and HE is funded by a different funding council.

The Dearing Committee report into higher education recommended that HEIs 'have in place a participation strategy, a mechanism for monitoring progress, and provision for review by the governing body of achievement' (Dearing, 1997, recommendation 3) and that the funding councils for F and HE collaborate strategically to fund work to widen participation across the two sectors. The HE funding councils have encouraged collaborative bidding for resources and, increasingly, partnerships between F and HE and employers are favoured in the allocation of funds.

Yet, a major gap which creates difficulties in ensuring success for many of these collaborative ventures is the lack of attention to the theory behind the policy initiatives producing misunderstandings and disagreements on future action (Edwards and Miller, 2000). In drawing together a concern for the level of social exclusion with a belief that widening participation in education is a 'good' idea, the suggestion is that education can effect a social revolution. It is increasingly the case that there are severe doubts as to whether this is a realistic aim of education itself. Yet, even if this premise is accepted, it is still important to be clear about how social inclusion can be achieved. One thread of the debate centres on the idea of 'ambassadors' who could return to communities to cele-brate their achievements and provide encouragement for others. The strategy to achieve this is to develop 'community leaders' (Duncan and Thomas, 2001), who, having received training, will be able to lead the way from exclusion to inclusion. This idea also lies at the heart of many of the current strategies for young people through the 'gifted and talented' schemes, which recommend that particular young people are targeted to develop their potential towards HE and then act as role models for others (DfEE, 2000, p 6). A policy that is based on individuals in this way remains a conservative approach to what purports to be a radical solution to participation in learning and society.

There are more collectivist theories that influence the dialectical concepts of inclusion/exclusion, in particular the notion of social capital (Coleman, 1994, Schuller and Field, 1998). The idea of social capital was originally espoused by Bourdieu, who identified the process of the accumulation and maintenance of power by the middle classes into other forms of capital beyond financial wealth to include cultural knowledges and social networks. Social capital theorists suggest that communities can be developed by supportive networks being fostered and encouraged through particular interventions such as education and joint approaches with other statutory and non-statutory agencies. Field (2000, p 149) suggests that the value of social capital approaches would be that inequalities could be overcome by creating '"bridging ties" that enable the least advantaged to access resources from outside their own ethnic, neighbourhood and kinship networks'. This could provide the resource power necessary to enable excluded groups to access the social benefits that they are often denied.

While there are significant possibilities here, especially if these networks of local people are able to control their use of resources, there still remain some concerns about any form of inclusionist approach, which Field also acknow-ledges. Preece (1999, p 10) says ideas of inclusion are based on 'normalising the unemployed or disaffected. As such it legitimates the status quo of those systems which might otherwise be regarded as contributing to the very problem being addressed.'

In other words, the inclusion/exclusion debate defines the problem of poverty, and lack of access to social and economic resources within communi-ties, in terms of the dysfunction of particular groups in those communities while failing to address the culpability of a system that maintains the status quo. The solution offered in this model is for these people to adjust to a taken-for-granted middle-class norm of behaviour, such as re-training, to enable inclusion in the benefits of middle-class life. Field (1999) notes that practitioners and researchers in the field of widening participation have not as yet realised the extent of coer-cion in the field of participation. He highlights the role of the New Deal but also says (1999, p 11):

> Without anyone much noticing, a great deal of professional development and skills updating is carried out not because anyone wants to learn or is ready to learn, but because they are required to learn … for a range of problems … the answer is to provide training, whether its subjects want it or not.

What is omitted from the inclusion/exclusion debate, what lies outside its parameters needs to be recognised as Preece (1999, p 13) points out:

> The new discourse of education recognises the problem of exclusion, but in addressing this problem as a cohesive project, makes some of the issues which constitute the problem, invisible – for example the issue of structural unemployment, the issue of age, the fact that some people are only indirectly contributing to the labour market as an intermediary between generations. Other unrecognised issues relate specifically to the nature of institutional provision and what counts as worthwhile learning. These issues question some of the assumptions that widening participation can be addressed by a linear and unproblematic strategy.

While I, like Preece, am criticising some of the thinking behind and absences within the notions of social exclusion/inclusion, I do not want to suggest that educational managers should abandon all attempts to widen participation or to further investigate attempts to empower marginalised individuals and groups. Indeed, the purpose of this book is to encourage a broad-ranging examination of the confusion that exists in the area of widening participation and to reflect on practice that has made a difference, however small, to individuals and communities in Britain. Rather, the point is that beneath what has been heralded as radical thinking is a strong conservative tendency grown out of taken-for-granted perceptions of acceptable social functions, which may actually reinforce previously failed practice. We need to take on new ways of thinking about education, communities and knowledge development if we are to be successful in this challenging project. Messages are contradictory, and while I have argued that the 'new' thinking since 1997, which emphasises collaboration and inclusion, is rooted in the 'old' thinking of 1992, I would also insist that the process of trying to encourage inclusivity in education is also producing a number of useful and innovative strategies in the field. Sitting alongside many of these developments is an older and more radical version of education provision, which has not been fully tapped as an effective resource. It is to this tradition I will now turn, showing how a more radical agenda, linked to a more strategic approach for widening participation, could create more successful interventions in the future.

Widening, or transformative, participation

Much of the debate about widening participation as a method of challenging exclusion has echoes of discussions within other educational debates about citizenship and education for a social purpose. Clearly, some of the work undertaken in further education in the 1970s and 1980s, particularly clustered in adult basic education (ABE) departments in FE, was both informed and influential in this movement. Equally, growing out of a more radical tradition of community-based education, a number of continuing education departments in universities have also argued for the development of learning programmes in partnership with industrial working class communities (Ward and Taylor, 1986).

During the 1980s, with the decline in the British manufacturing base, this work took on a particular political focus (Francis, 1989; Trotman and Lewis, 1990) and included work with mining communities during and beyond the miners' strike (Reynolds, 1995), other trade union groups (Forrester, 1995) and with women's groups through second-wave feminism and the peace movement, producing a growth in women's education programmes and 'peace studies'. These developments influenced many academic disciplines by encouraging a re-examination of the contribution of women to the parameters of knowledge (Delmar, 1986, Thompson, 1983, 1995). Edwards (1997) has suggested that while there are different roots to widening participation, only one has genuine radical roots, the social purpose model, but he also points out that this model has had little impact on the mainstream of F and HE policy. Most of the work undertaken by colleagues within the social purpose tradition was marginal to the main business of FE colleges and universities. There are, however, lessons that can be learnt from marginal activity that can both challenge practice and provide alternative models of action, and indeed management, to access groups and individuals who have been alienated from the mainstream of society.

A central component of the social purpose model of widening participation to education is a belief that citizens' rights are secured through action and learning. Calls for an education for citizenship (Advisory Group on Citizenship, 1998), across school, further and higher education are beginning to have an impact. Citizenship is a contested and shifting concept. It is not a fixed state. It was the previous Conservative government that talked about 'the enemy within', re-defining who had citizenship rights. Currently, the debate about asylum seekers re-opens the debate about citizenship and the nature of British society. Equally in the EU and the US, definitions of citizenship are increasingly an area of contention for governments. Like the notion of education, citizenship can be exclusive. Inclusion within society can be used as a threat to limit the citizenship rights of others (you are in, you are not) and create boundaries, which simulta-neously include and exclude, around particular communities. Citizens' rights need to be won by critiquing taken-for-granted notions of entitlement, as Martin (1999, p 90) points out:

> There is a venerable tradition of adult education and adult learning which has always been about struggle ... to democratise democracy. This tradition which exists in varying forms in different national and cultural contexts ... reflects a view about lifelong learning that has been concerned consistently to connect learning with living in the fullest sense of that word ... Citizenship and democracy in this sense have to be made and remade all the time. This is as much an educational task as a political one.

In other words, any real engagement with inclusion requires an education for citizenship. Johnston (1999) reflects on different models of citizenship, suggesting that there is a need to recognise learning for different aspects of citi-zenship: inclusive citizenship; pluralistic citizenship; reflexive citizenship; and active citizenship – each bearing a different relationship to the rights of a citizen and their position in the society. Learning across the lifespan would need to be a pre-requisite for active citizenship. This typology of citizenship is useful in identifying what is problematic about the current rhetoric about widening participation. It seems that while politicians, funders and managers of further and higher education embrace 'widening participation', what they are embracing is only focused on one form of participation, akin to inclusive citizenship, as Johnston describes it or, as Martin (1999, p 92) puts it: 'in a democratic learning society education for active citizenship has to be about not simply how to be a citizen (i.e. inclusion or fitting in) but rather about deciding what being a citizen should mean.'

From this perspective, participation in education continues to be focused on fitting people into what is already available, rather than encouraging them to contribute to the development of education thinking. Perhaps the concept of active participation or a participation that allows critique is more useful for a radical approach to the development of the post-16 education sectors. Implicit in the idea of changing notions of citizenship is a belief in difference and different knowledges within a society. This is not to say that there is no truth but simply that truth is contextual and that sophisticated understandings and interpretations of knowledge do not always only reside in the established institutions of society such as the academy but may be found in different communities. In attempting to widen participation in F and HE, we need to be sure that the knowledge being offered is relevant and open to critique by the communities who are being included. This is perhaps the most significant challenge to post-16 education but it does not automatically come from the education participation debate. Connecting debates on citizenship and social advocacy for citizenship rights questions our knowledge, not about what already exists, but rather about what might be, and re-focuses a radical vision for participation across the sector.

At the heart of a radical approach to widening participation has to be an evaluation of curriculum and a recognition that learning cannot be contained by institutions and indeed that educational establishments cannot simply solve issues of poverty and access to resources. To quote Martin again (1999, p 93):

> Although social exclusion must be central to the agenda of the democratic learning society, it is not a problem which is amenable to educational solutions alone. We should avoid treating 'education as the waste paper basket of social policy' (Halsey, 1972) a repository for dealing with social problems where solutions are uncertain or where there is a disinclination to wrestle with them seriously.

To engage in a social purpose perspective on widening participation requires educationalists to re-conceive their position within society. Here, educationalists are asked not only to take on the economic imperative for a more educated workforce or to address issues of social cohesion but to work with communities and the people who live within those communities to engage in a dialogue of knowledge creation, rather than what is. This requires working together with different and new partners engaged in the development often of unknown territory. This kind of work has always been marginal activity for large organisations such as F and HE institutions and it is perhaps an essential component of this style of practice that it remains marginal. However, taking on board lessons that can be learnt from this work would require a significant shift in the organisation and structures of post-16 education and affect change both within and beyond F and HE. Post-16 education is in crisis, both financially and in understanding its purpose in a post-modern, post-industrial society. Exploring alternatives born out of radical marginal traditions could provide opportunities to examine different ways of working, developing new forms of alliances and partnerships and help the sector to re-think its position in a changing society.

This chapter has examined the different perspectives on widening participation in current discourse in post-16 education. It has suggested that claims that widening participation is necessarily radical are not valid and that to enable any form of widening participation requires managers in the sectors to change practice and engage their organisations in new ways of working. The themes of competition, inclusion and transformative participation are developed further in the rest of the book. The next chapter examines how a management process can take forward the change required to widen access and participation in F and HE.

Note

1. Education for all did not, of course, include a substantial section of the population, especially disabled children and those with learning difficulties. For further discussion on this point see my chapter in Leicester, M and Field, J (2000) *Lifelong Learning: Learning Across the Lifespan*, London: Routledge/Falmer.

3 Development, management and innovative practice

> Management (like teaching) is coming to be seen as a professional skill calling for initial and updating education rather than just a natural talent. The dynamics and micropolitics of organisational change however remain under-researched and little theorised in the field (Duke, 1994, p 223).

This chapter examines management in F and HE. It discusses the process of management, the difficulty of managing in F and HE and suggests how change management can be used to facilitate a widening participation agenda. It argues that widening participation requires a different management style to conventional approaches and it suggests that collaboration between managers and their teams is a more fruitful way of organising practice for widening participation activities. In order to facilitate a vibrant and developing organisation, all participants should be able to contribute to the functioning of the organisation. Certainly any organisation requires visionaries and it is the case that these people can often be managers, although, of course, this is not necessarily the case.

Management operates at different levels and managing projects and activities within projects is equally important to the overall management of organisations. Learning from practice, in particular from activities that are at the margins of organisations, will offer the innovation and creativity needed to enable widening participation to F and HE in the future. Government is increasingly taking a managerial stance in an attempt to control the progress towards achieving its vision of widening participation. I suggest that government's approach to leading widening participation will affect how managers in educational institutions respond to developments in the sector. Throughout the chapter, I highlight the need for partnership to facilitate change, between not only staff and their managers, but also between students, researchers in the field, funding councils, government and institutions. I begin by setting out current government thinking, which determines the agenda that managers in the sector have to address. I argue that the role of government and its agents in the management of educational institutions should be recognised explicitly as part of a new partnership between government and the sector.

Widening participation and joined-up thinking

Historically, governments have used their overall control of public sector organisations to further their vision for the society that they govern. Governments have influenced public services by controlling the allocation of budgets through intermediary organisations such as funding councils and local and regional government. It is obvious, but worth noting, that in thinking about management in a public sector organisation it is vital to be aware of the social and political context in which the organisation is framed.

At any time in the public sector, policy decisions and changes provide a series of frameworks which managers use to create their own local practice. Current policies in Britain emphasise one core principle, the expansion of the sectors to *include* a broader base of learners. This principle is also evident globally and is rooted in economic changes. The strategic framework set out by the British government broadly accords with principles set out in international policy statements like *Learning, the Treasure Within* (Delors, 1996) and *Lifelong Learning for All* (OECD, 1996). Hence, developments in Britain are part of a new emerging global strategy for post-initial education that is concerned with 'global economic competition, the knowledge or information revolution, the fragmentation of society and culture, and threats to public order of the widening gap between rich and poor, increasingly defined as social inclusion and exclusion' (Griffin, 1999, p 12).

The main approach in Britain has been to develop strategies to widen participation in our further and higher education institutions. At the heart of this strategy lies a belief in 'joined-up thinking' whereby a range of agencies are encouraged to work together to enable diverse learners to develop their capacity to contribute effectively to society. While the crude determinant of budget allocation has been refined and government and funding bodies use funding as a tool, there are also other mechanisms which are now being used to encourage widening access and participation across the sector. These tools form a management framework with four main elements: strategic thinking, standards, regionalisation and evidence-based practice. In this section, I examine each of these four areas and discuss how they affect decisions taken in F and HE.

Strategic thinking

As argued in Chapter 2, the 1992 F and HE Act in Britain did achieve a significant increase in the number of people taking up post-16 learning opportunities. Massification, in the general sense, has been substantially achieved. However, current government strategy, while continuing the policy of massification – aiming for 50 per cent of under 30-year-olds to have some sort of higher education qualification by 2010 (DfEE, 2000, p 3) – is more especially focused on widening participation for inclusion, focusing on groups who are particularly under-represented in the sector:

> It is critical that more of our young people who come from families with no higher education in their backgrounds are able to enter universities and other HEIs ... At present only 28 per cent of entrants to higher

education are from disadvantaged backgrounds (social classes III-manual, IV and V) (DfEE, 2000, p 3).

Increasingly, the term 'strategy' is becoming more significant than the concept of 'policy' in government planning for social affairs, as Griffin (1999) notes. He points out that, 'there is a historic movement away from state policy formation and planning towards government strategy' (Griffin, 1999, p 12). In other words, the consequences of highlighting the failure of earlier welfarist policies, which focused on the end goal of equality, has meant that current governments are more interested in the means or strategy by which inclusion is achieved. In Britain, government is shifting its emphasis from a more hands-off policy approach to a more interventionist strategy approach. Government ministers are increasingly acting more like chief executives who determine 'how to' achieve rather than just 'what to' achieve.

Focusing on the means or strategy to achieve targets is a different way of managing. Strategy highlights plans and measures to test the success of plans. It requires baseline information to be able (later) to evaluate how far the strategic aims have been achieved. Strategic planning has been important in many organisations for quite some time but the crucial difference in the current climate is that institutions are increasingly being expected to demonstrate and share their 'strategies' to receive funding.

FE has been subject to such regimes since the process of incorporation but more recently the HE funding councils have required a plethora of strategies from HEIs. While the funding councils for HE are disinclined to move from being 'funders' to being planners and certainly managers in the sector are generally resisting this shift, it is happening. Annual operating statements are more proscribed and, increasingly, even funding for staff recruitment and retention is subject to acceptable Human Resources 'strategies'. In the field of widening participation, the HE funding councils requested widening participation statements from institutions in 1999. Storan (2001, p 2) draws out the key elements in the advice to institutions:

> Guidance provided ... proposed seven areas for inclusion in the initial statements: aims and objectives and mechanisms for achieving these, the relationship of how these objectives related to institutional mission, a profile of the present and potential student population, identification of under-represented groups with targets for improvement, summary of student retention approaches, indicators that the institution would use to monitor progress, identification of key partners and collaborative arrangements to implement the strategy.

The key unstated point of this approach was to move widening participation activities from being marginal activities conducted by enthusiasts to being a central focus for all institutions. Senior managers were expected to be accountable for targets set and detail progress towards increased participation. Increasingly, formula funding, which has been a feature of FE for some time, with specifically earmarked pots of money for widening participation, is now part of the strategy to encourage widening participation in HE. At the heart of the government's approach to widening participation is an attempt to engage the total vision of an organisation, and to see widening participation as part of the development of the whole institution. Government, therefore, is expecting institutions to devise their own approach to widening participation within a framework of targets and centrally produced criteria.

Further education colleges, like universities, are expected to bid for funds to develop initiatives. The LSC is more directly a planning organisation than its predecessor the Further Education Funding Council. The LSC has set targets, which they relay to colleges by establishing criteria for funding. While at one level this approach provides a method of change in the sector, it does skew the direction of widening participation towards a simple achievement of targets, which inevitably favours crude number games rather than the more challenging and difficult-to-quantify active engagement approach. In other words, it favours creating 'deficit individuals and communities' that can be identified, targeted and then developed to indicate success. Managers in educational institutions now need to assess their own involvement in widening participation in the light of government demands for information, targets and measures of success, as the process of agreeing and assessing is now common in both F and HE.

The second element of the government's vision for widening participation is, ironically, standards.

Standards

While David Blunkett was the Secretary of State for Education, he highlighted the importance of standards in discussing the strategy on failing schools. He said 'We are beginning to improve schools in areas that have been neglected for so long that the eulogies to equality of opportunity rang rather hollow' (Blunkett, 2000).

To enable the development of widening participation, standards need to be set, measured and maintained. This approach lies at the heart of continuing government policy, exemplified by the *Excellence Challenge* (DfEE, 2000) where the main focus was on raising attainment in schools. In the language of widening participation, the vocabulary of standards has become important. We use the term 'standards' as if it has a clear universal meaning. Language is not fixed, different people will mean different things when they use the same language and the concept of standards is not neutral. Currently, the term standards is connected with ideas of quality, effectiveness and measurement, measurement that is rooted in league tables, determined by GCSE and A level scores which produce sound-bite results where schools can be judged as 'effective' or 'failing'. For colleges and universities, the regime of inspection produces a fear of failure, which can induce change, but this is often a negative style of management.

The standards debate directly affects the sector's ability to engage with more radical notions of widening participation. The league tables that each year are studied wearily by Vice Chancellors and Principals and that dominate the broadsheets place greater emphasis on A-level entry points than any other criteria, which disadvantages the new universities who have had a better track record in recruiting a more diverse student base. Equally, this also this militates against the old university sector being more flexible about recognising different student experience on entry to HE. FE colleges have consistently received poorer ratings for their HE-level work often simply because of under resourcing, and this structural fact does not assist in the process of widening participation. As one college principal told me:

> what you have is a government that is sending out mixed messages, saying we wish to widen participation and tackle social exclusion and colleges are the place we can do that but that doesn't sit easily with a funding regime that gives more to school sixth forms than to other provision and decisions to create more sixth forms and so on ... I don't want to make too much of this but it is an issue because it throws up difficulties for collaboration; why should the head of a sixth form collaborate with the college? These are not people who don't care about their students, they do, but what is in it for them? They have to care about their staff and so on, too. I suspect that in giving to some very powerful interest groups the government has jeopardised the widening participation agenda (Seaside College Principal, 2000).

Rather than learning the lessons of the access debate on adult learning of the 1970s and 1980s (Thompson, 1983), the current emphasis on standards and measurements will continue to exclude people from learning opportunities and require ongoing development of adult learning for those who were excluded. FE is consistently seen as a lesser partner in its provision because sixth form colleges are more successful in standards' terms and therefore the students who have been brought into further education are less valued as future learners. This is not to argue that examining how far conventional systems can be adapted to enable more diverse learners to participate beyond school is not a sensible idea, but it is simply to point out that one consequence of mainstreaming widening participation, rather than changing the system, has been to try to make diverse learners fit into current practice, and to fit learners into current criteria for success. As Field (2000, p 135) points out:

> If the consequences of a learning society are as momentous as they appear, it makes no sense whatever to plan and manage schooling as though nothing has changed. Yet that is, for the most part, what seems to be happening ... some would like school to become a bastion of traditional values and establishment certainties.

The more challenging work to engage diverse learners in further and higher education does continue but it is largely project funded and marginal. The challenge for managers, both government and local managers, is to find ways to draw this work within overall organisational development and to develop standards that offer more diverse measures that recognise success in difference.

The third part of the government's framework for widening participation is rooted in a belief that working in partnership within a region is a more effective way of developing inclusion.

Regionalisation

For government, and many in the sector, there is a recognition that for a large proportion of the population learning needs to be local. There is extensive evidence and understanding that any part-time learning will not be attractive to new learners if it is beyond a distance that people are comfortable travelling. Equally, full-time HE students from poorer socio-economic groups and from many minority ethnic groups do not feel comfortable, or are able to afford, being very far from their home. Government has, therefore, increasingly identified regional and local approaches to widening participation as a vital component to achieve success. They are increasingly funding colleges, and more controversially, universities through a regional structure. FE is now funded via a regional structure of branches of the Learning and Skills Council. HE funding is channelled through the Scottish, English and Welsh funding councils which have some different priorities. Although the bulk of HE funding for England comes from a central English funding council, widening participation projects are funded through regional HE funding. The LSC also focuses on the development of a strategic framework with local priorities to be set and achieved. Strategy and standards are developed within a regional framework, as Gravatt (2000, p 35) highlights when talking about the Learning and Skills Council:

> The new council ... funds a vast sector, covering both schools and small companies, yet to do so with simpler systems at a regional level. They expect the funding system to deliver growth in participation and achievement, to be responsive to individuals and employers and to implement equal opportunities. They expect a national tariff to be drawn up with four types of unit, covering entry, retention, achievement and disadvantage – the last covering both social and educational disadvantage.

Equally important to increased regional funding is a belief in and commitment to regional and local partnerships. Working in partnership with others is discussed in detail in the next chapter. However, in FE local links have been a major feature of management from their initial development, first with local authorities and more recently, with incorporation, with businesses. The Ufi, or LearnDirect, which provides learning packages, often e-learning based, is regionally located and is managed by consortia of colleges and businesses. Work with local communities and the voluntary sector has been patchier but has increased as the emphasis on collaboration and social justice has resurfaced in recent years. In HE, the picture is less instrumental but institutions do see their links regionally and locally as significant, as Watson and Taylor (1998, p 115) point out: 'Virtually all universities refer in their institutional plans to the need for good relations and partnerships with their local communities, although only 47 per cent of traditional universities regard this as a high priority compared with 74 per cent of new universities.'

Working in partnership within a region does offer exciting possibilities for widening participation but it also presents challenges. Partnership must not be viewed simply as one type of activity and the nature of the partnership will affect the process and the outcomes of the activities; but for joined-up thinking, regional working and working together is taken for granted. This is clearly evident in the new plans for the development of the jointly-funded, HEFCE and Learning and Skills Council (LSC) 'Partnerships for Progression' (2001). Because partnership is seen to be the most important element of enabling widening participation in post-16 education, the next chapter details the complex nature of partnerships and discusses the different elements required for effective partnership working. Clearly, these different elements present challenges for managers in the sector. Increasingly the funders are becoming more interventionist in their approach and managers are being required to negotiate their organisational strategy in a more prescribed climate.

The final element of government strategy is an approach that is rooted in learning from research.

Evidence-based practice

For quite some time within the field of health and social care, and increasingly in education, the notion of evidence-based practice has become a significant contributor to government strategy to produce change. Based in a notion of 'what works' or as Desforges calls it 'what worked' (2000, p 9), it highlights research and the sharing of 'good practice'. Within the field of widening participation, evidence-based practice is the final element of government strategy to develop inclusion in the post-16 sector. It is an area of strategy that potentially could provide innovation for practice. It is also a form of partnership between funders, co-ordinating or research teams and institutions. In further education, as well as providing space for collaboration, Learning Partnerships have a remit to 'reach out into local communities and find out what it is that local people really need' (Lifelong Learning Partnerships, 2000). The information gathered will be fed back to the regional level of the LSC. Good practice data is stored on the partnerships' website. Research and 'what works' are now central elements in developing new partnerships for learning. Increasingly colleges are being encouraged to engage in their own evidence-based practice (Martinez, 2001) and the Learning and Skills Development Agency (LSDA)'s recent work has focused much more specifically on such research. Good practice guides have been produced by the funding councils, for example *Strategies for Widening Participation in Higher Education* (HEFCE, 2001a). A network of national support and co-ordinating groups for HE widening participation activities has also been established. This includes groups such as Action on Access, the Access Advisory Partnership and the National Disability Team whose remit is to draw together good practice without an 'inspection culture', although some have a monitoring function. To take just one example of this process, Action on Access was appointed by the HEFCE as a national co-ordination team for widening participation in January 2000. It has two major roles in that it supports both individual projects and institutional strategic development in widening participation. The project support is for the HEFCE/Learning and Skills Council widening participation initiatives in both HEIs and FE colleges. The projects are organised on a regional basis and have a focus both on the needs of the region and the institution. The other major aspect of Action on Access's work is in supporting HEIs in the development of widening participation strategic developments.

Based at the University of Bradford, this national co-ordinating team draws in expertise from across the country. The team not only provides support to projects and institutions but also disseminates good practice across the country, helping isolated projects to learn from more general data.

The co-ordinator of the Action on Access team told me:

> I think we've got a wonderful opportunity ... There is the opportunity to really make something quite big out of the way HEFCE's approached the whole area. You've got some formula funding, you've got to do something about your mainstream activity through that and you've got some project money which is about risk and innovation and you should go away and play with it and develop nice things and tell us about them. Don't be worried if you [make mistakes] just tell us about what happened. It's about powerful opportunities ... to dabble, and what we have to make sure is that that has a major voice within the sector ... It is a tremendous opportunity to spend time to identify the strengths and the weaknesses ... and say this is what we mean to do to change the sector ... We've got the opportunity to change the measuring tools; our measuring tools are all around percentage of 2.1s, A-level points, staff–student ratio, and how many people complete their degree within five years, well so what? Look down the league table and try and pull out something that is about social inclusion; oh we've suddenly got a new 'stat' that's about social inclusion. Well, hang on a minute it's like a bolt-on extra-mural department, we've got to change the whole basis of those performance indicators ... It's giving practitioners the opportunity to get in there (2000).

He went on to point out the advantages of a national co-ordination team that are made up of people rooted in practice, rather than policy makers, who can share knowledge with colleagues:

> I think it is important, let me give you an example ... There is an area of deprivation in terms of disadvantage that's coming out of projects. It's regionally based but is starting to come out of the national work, which is the coastline across the whole of Britain has high deprivation indicators. You go down the coastline, all the way down the east coast, down the south coast, to south west, then Wales, then up north, and you have groupings of people with limited opportunities and poor participation and even when they are surrounded by rich affluent regions ... and you start to say well, now we've identified that, what can we do about it?
>
> From a regional perspective you may have picked up isolated bits but not seen the whole picture and we've also got things that are happening in different parts of the country that are relevant to other parts that can be shared. Take Yorkshire and the Humber. It's not a particularly

homogenous region ... well, Scarborough's a bit different to the steel industry in Sheffield or the textile mills of Bradford. The cultures are miles apart and this idea that there is a unitary region is imaginary ... We need to learn from other projects that deal with similar cultures, even if they are in different parts of the country ... You might even been able to do some real comparative studies. I think that has been a major problem with some of the initiatives as you go back to previous projects, there was no connectivity.

Projects have been managed and developed by isolated practitioners who have very little authority within institutions and I think that there is actually a seismic shift. The emphasis is now far more on structured change across institutions (2000).

Nevertheless, members of the Action on Access team were not unaware of the challenges in achieving real widening participation across the sectors. One team member told me:

I am not sure how deeply widening participation runs in institutions. We underestimate the university sector and opposition runs deeper than people care to believe. So I am not convinced that the kinds of reforms in funding are sufficient in terms of the amount of change required. There is a political problem for the funding council because we know, against what people say, that when they talk about diversity what they mean is that there are elite institutions and there are other institutions. So diversity in the sector can mean you accept that you could see widening participation as broadening the gap between those institutions that are serious about widening participation and the others that are not. I do not know if five per cent premium is sufficient funding incentive to push the reluctant into taking it seriously ... They have other income streams that are much more significant. That is why I think if there is a real desire and funding is a key way of doing that then this five per cent incentive isn't enough. It matters in some institutions because the margin of money can make a difference but if I was sitting in another institution I would be thinking that we have other income from the RAE and so on. But I guess that is where we can come in, through Action on Access, and tell the funding councils they are not doing enough. It's about a dialogue (2000).

All four of the elements of government strategy favour an inclusivist version of widening participation which is mainstreamed across institutions, as discussed in the previous chapter. However recognising the value of more marginal activity, such as project work, where innovative practice can develop needs greater attention. Evidence-based practice needs to be critically evaluated and not thought to provide ultimate solutions to difficult problems. It is possible to see some of these co-ordinating groups as intermediaries who can advocate for change through the funding councils, the DfES and within institutions. Working with such groups can be a useful tactic for managers at any level in their institutions who want relevant change, as groups like this can provide expertise and knowledge to facilitate development within organisations.

Governments and their intermediaries are more closely involved than ever in local decision making across the sector. Managers in institutions will need to engage critically with an inclusivist view of widening participation whatever their own perspective. This creates difficulties for institutions that have diverse missions – a problem that is particularly acute in higher education but which also affects further education.

In this section, I have examined the framework determined by government and their intermediaries which sets out the parameters within which managers in further and higher education work. I have discussed how government is a central part of managing in F and HE and highlighted how their frameworks both constrain and offer possibilities for mangers in institutions. Following on from the role of government in widening participation, I now turn my attention to the process of managing F and HE and suggest that for many, historically, this process has been ambiguous.

The problem with managing

When I was asked to take on the role of Pro Vice Chancellor, I found myself intensely embarrassed when talking to colleagues who were practitioners. A friend of mine, a lecturer in Sociology at a university in South Africa, commented that he didn't really know what Pro Vice Chancellors did, but he was very anti Vice Chancellors! I confess to jokingly saying to colleagues, 'Oh well, I've really sold out now'. I did that because, as Harper (1997, p 38) says referring to FE: 'Many people … perceive leaders or managers as foes rather than friends. They perceive them as "collaborators" with the new forces of managerialism invading the autonomy traditionally enjoyed in FE.'

Pritchard (2000, p 16) also identifies this tendency, resulting specifically from the 1992 F and HE Act. He says 'Viewed from the perspective of the lecturer, senior post-holders have been largely complicit in articulating a "hard" uncompromising top-down managerialism that has invariably turned colleges into battlegrounds.'

While these comments are specifically referring to further education, the distrust of management is equally strong in higher education and in many ways the changes taking place in further and higher education mean that management processes are increasingly converging. It is the case that 'although their roles may differ to some extent, the issues they face are very similar' (Phillips, 1995, p 159). However, it is also not always clear what the role of an academic manager is and, as Slowey (1995, p 28) points out, 'organising academics is … akin to herding cats'.

The distrust and the development of a 'them and us' culture between management and workers in F and HE is largely dysfunctional to new initiatives and innovation. Wherever the new ideas spring from, the 'other side' will be distrustful of the motivation of the initiator. The nature of the work in the F and HE sector encourages scepticism and a challenging and independent approach to our work environment. This is an important part of the field and needs to be acknowledged both by managers and their teams.

Among many people who work in the field of widening participation, the notion of management cuts across democratic processes that they have been used to in community settings. On the other hand, those who are more used to notions of accountable leadership would argue that entirely democratic decision making is often too slow to address the requirements of change at the speed necessary in the new world of organisations. Whatever the ins and outs of the debate, the reality for many workers in F and HE is that management, especially in the climate of competition that was fostered during the 1990s as discussed in the previous chapter, is distrusted. As Stanley (1998, p 2) commented when talking about the Kennedy (1997) and Dearing (1996) reports:

> Disappointingly, Kennedy seems blithely unaware of the Genghis Khan nature of the management of much of further education, the exploited staff and worsening employment conditions ... Equally disappointingly, Dearing seems not to have moved beyond surface generalities in examining what goes on in higher education, what aspects have changed and in what ways, what the impact of perpetual funding cuts have been. The result is that neither seems to know what 'education' actually consists of in further education and higher education in the later 1990s.

Many staff in F and HE still find the style of management developed in colleges and universities during the 1990s to be alien to their beliefs and removed from their practice. It is also alien to the development of widening participation. However, as Duke (1994) points out, unless we investigate and explore the processes involved in managing, much of our scepticism of management remains based on limited research and particular prejudices.

All members of the F and HE communities need to take management seriously and work to develop a style of management that works with different experience, both the difference that is thrown up by increasing participation to under represented students and the differences that exists among the people who work in the sector. In the next section, I propose a different approach to managing in F and HE.

Re-defining management – collaboration and partnership

Many of the old structures and practices within F and HE have not delivered a significantly more diverse post-16 student population. If we are to alter the composition and culture of our post-16 education system to include a wider range of learners, then change is necessary (Adams, 2001) and it is important that this process of change is managed effectively and collaboratively. Stanley (1998) is right to point out that there is a genuine need to reconfigure the culture of management in F and HE. Management needs to be reconceptualised to accommodate and learn from the diversity that the widening participation in education proposes. Styles of management need to encompass and facilitate creativity in staff. Staff in educational institutions bring with them a wealth of experience, from their backgrounds, their personal circumstances and from their social, cultural and civic responsibilities. Tapping these resources will release substantial energy and knowledge to meet the challenges of education in the twenty-first century.

Leaders and their team members need to develop greater clarity about the process of management and the organisational change necessary to facilitate widening participation. Management in F and HE should not only reflect the needs of managers but also should grow out of the purpose and activities of students, and potential students, as well as the workers in an organisation. This suggests that managers need to know about their team and work with them to be clear about what they do, how they get things done and how their work can be developed. Staff need to recognise that their experience beyond the work environment may well be useful to the new age of education, and connections between their life experiences and those of their students and potential students will increase the power of this new alignment of educational practice. This is the second form of partnership that I see as significant to enable change, a partnership between all the parties in educational institutions. This requires a different approach to organisational change, one that is rooted in a multi-faceted communication system and knowledge exchange, where individuals and groups work together in partnership to create and implement the vision of the organisation based on a shared understanding of the educational and social environment.

Management is a process-driven system, the totality of how we 'get things done'. It needs to be understood to operate at different levels, strategically, taking account of both internal and external forces, and operationally, whether project- or activity-based.

Management is not leadership. Leadership is a component of the management process and leaders are important to 'getting things done' but so are activists who 'do' what is required. Leadership is about vision, motivation and direction, or enabling things to get done. Using a partnership approach to management facilitates good leadership, as Bass (1981, p 45) points out: 'the real test of leadership lies not in the personality or behaviour of the leaders, but in the performance of the groups they lead.' Defining management as a partnership suggests that all workers in an organisation contribute to the process of management and change, no matter how marginal they are. The next section looks at the process of change management in organisations and how managers can develop this process creatively.

Managing for the future

F and HE institutions need to change their practice with students and their communities if they are going to widen the base of their student population but they also need to change practices between staff, highlighting the role of management as a collaborative approach to 'getting things done' and also to developing new activity. This is a process of continual reflection on activities. As Duke points out, change is inherent to organisations. He says (1994, p 223): 'It is clear however that no organisation is static ... change has become a constant factor, management all but equated with development.' This approach will require participants to feel sufficiently secure to live with change and for trust between staff to grow out of clarity of purpose, good two-way communication systems and a genuine sharing of information and knowledge.

Many institutions have now developed a range of mechanisms that are attracting more new students into study, but recruitment can be achieved by activities that need not affect the whole of the institution as the activities for recruitment may well be marginal to the organisation. Retaining students on the other hand requires whole organisational change management. The organisation needs to adapt to the needs of its new student groups. This is not just the responsibility of managers but should be developed by the whole of the organisation. Seeing management as an inclusive process where all staff need to contribute is the most realistic approach to enable organisations to develop effectively in the constantly and rapidly changing world of education. Education organisations focus specifically on knowledge transition and knowledge development, therefore management in F and HE must support these broad aims. The challenge lies in enabling a diverse group of people, students and potential students to be able to participate in the dialogue about knowledge. A massification perspective on widening participation would suggest that the change required would entail larger class sizes, the use of new technologies and a greater emphasis on diverse learning modes. An inclusivist approach would also emphasise the development of learning support systems and more diverse learning and teaching styles, while a more active participation approach would encourage all of the above as well as a re-evaluation of knowledge and knowledge production including new curricula areas and a more permeable approach to learning itself. Managing widening participation cannot simply be about targets but requires a more organic approach to change. To succeed, collaborative management processes, which highlight communication and information sharing between all staff, are vital.

The process of change to create an education fit for the purposes of a postmodern/post-industrial/late-capitalist information society requires some elements of stepping into the unknown. Tanner argues that successful organisations are more adaptive and that in thinking about development within organisations, being comfortable with uncertainty is important. He says (1990, p 108):

> When disruption occurs, our managerial response is generally to impose order as quickly as possible. The old mindset is predicated on the virtues of stability. Organisations are structured to reduce ambiguity ...
> stability can be defined as the capacity of a system to return to equilibrium after it has been disrupted, the more rapidly it returns, the less it fluctuates and the more stable it is. Resilience may be viewed as the 'measure of the persistence of a system and its ability to absorb change and disturbance'. Resilience entails the ability to continue to function to survive, to absorb disturbance. Resilience entails an adaptive strategy not a stabilising one.

Senior managers have the responsibility to manage the development of the organisation's strategy. This entails a need for managers to interpret government policy in the context of their organisation and locale. Educational institutions have often used gatekeeping as a way of identifying the transition of knowledge. They are structured to encourage this process but if widening participation is to become a reality, the challenge for change management is to re-think how knowledge transition can be developed in a less exclusive structure. This may sound like a philosophical detail but it has a practical point. The question of knowledge must lie at the heart of any education system, and rather than widening participation being about including more and different groups of people in institutions of knowledge, we need to now examine what knowledge is important in what context and how best to transmit it.

It is all too often the case that good practice is abandoned in order to facilitate change. Managers need to think carefully about what needs to change and what needs to stay the same (Smale, 1996, p 51). Introducing a dialogue with staff across the institution, as well as with students and potential students, will enable managers to gain a better sense of what change is required. As Smale (1996, p 57) says:

> We need to look at the key players: those people whose actions will determine whether an innovation is adopted. From this analysis the change agent will be able to identify what sort of action needs to be taken with whom, to plan the transactions that have to be undertaken to manage the adoption of the innovation.

Working with all the key players in the process enables all staff to see they are part of the change:

> The key factor identified here for successfully managing change with a large diverse institution is to seek to take people at all levels with you ... The challenge is to make sure that the staff feel involved, that they are contributing to the process, that they own the concept, but at the same time to play down any talk that there is a process of change taking place. It is only on reflection that people will realise the extent of the change which has taken place because they were so much part of the process (Layer, 1995, p 124).

It is a senior manager's responsibility to oversee the development of new initiatives and to smooth the transition for staff and students through change. This is the role of strategy, the 'how to get there' element of development. For Harper, the key to this process is communication. She says (1997, p 40): 'The most effective form of communicating change involves talking to people formally and informally, encouraging questions, telling the truth and allowing people to express their feelings.'

Communication will not always be easy and teams and individuals within organisations will hold different views about new developments. Tallantyre (1995, p 107) highlights that this means that at any stage of development there will be a spectrum of positions on the change process:

Change works when you move along the spectrum from 'enthusiastic to emergent and through to unwilling modernisers'. The enthusiastic were able to fully engage with developments and provide good models for transfer, the emergent could become convinced of the feasibility and work at a more cautious pace.

Shifting an organisation's focus towards widening participation will often not be as alien to many in the organisation if managers work with staff and draw on the wealth of experience they hold:

In practice, many people within the institution were already committed to playing a central role in the region and to an informal view of the educational process. Some were school or college governors, others had children at local schools or colleges. It was an important first step to use the experience and commitment of these people to tackle the prejudices of the few who felt that contact with further education was not appropriate for a university (King, 1995, p 45).

It is, therefore, important to work with colleagues from their own starting point and recognise their networks and knowledge. This will make the process easier and more real for the institution, but it is also important to identify the key staff who will be enthusiasts for change. It is worth quoting King again:

One also needs a great deal of luck and the ability to find and keep good people to make the change happen. They are the real agents of change. These people are part of a wide network which reaches beyond the university walls in colleges, school, amongst unemployed women attending courses or chief executives attending meetings.

Each situation is different and the change agents need flexible and powerful antennae to read the predominant language and cultural norms (1995, p 49).

The reality for many lecturers in F and HE is that they feel overstretched, and if managers suggest change as something extra rather than something significantly different, the change is not likely to be well received. The most significant issue in change management processes is clarity of purpose between the different members of the organisation, developed through good communication and information sharing. It requires an iteration between senior managers and their staff and needs on-going attention. As Martinez (2001, p 26) highlights:

Leadership to raise achievement is not merely concerned with planning and starting activity where change is significant, senior managers will need to provide continuing support and pressure ... until the change is embedded.

In this section, I have discussed the need for change to facilitate the widening participation agenda in organisations and I have highlighted some of the difficulties and, I hope, solutions to achieving that change. I have identified the key elements of the change process and in the next section, I discuss the importance of marginal activities to enable innovative approaches to widening participation.

The role of marginality in change management

In Chapter 2, I pointed out that one area of particular significance that has often been neglected in managing change and innovation is the role of marginal activities in organisations. These activities operate at the interface between the groups and individuals who have been alienated from education and the institutions. This interface can shed light on organisational practices that are often taken for granted. Marginal activity can also allow organisations to test out new developments and provide valuable opportunities to develop new practice.

Traditionally, widening participation activities have been developed by enthusiastic individuals and groups who largely work with people outside their institution, and their work has been marginal to the mainstream of the institution. Funding for such activity is often found from alternative sources to the main funders of the sector, or the money has been short-term pump-priming funding. While there are severe disadvantages to this type of approach, particularly because much of the work of widening participation needs long-term development, it is also the case that being marginal to the mainstream of institutions allows greater flexibility to develop new ways of working. It provides examples of contrasting and complementary approaches to engaging new learners and agencies. These new approaches are invaluable to development, as Smale (1996, p 59) insists 'Marginality is crucial so that the change agent can see other people's perspectives.'

People who work on the margins will have a different focus to those who work solely within the centre of an organisation. This difference is particularly crucial to any period of re-conception of purpose in an organisation, because their perspective of the organisation will be more distanced, drawing on outsiders' view of the institution. Marginality also provides institutions with a resource of different contacts for widening participation as marginal workers will always develop support networks outside their institutions:

> Both internal and external networks are essential components of a
> strong development programme, giving support to the risk-takers and
> attracting the interest of the cautious. People who are marginal tend to
> join networks (Hawkins and Winter, 1997, p 22).

Institutions often do not use the resource of marginality and in fact it is sometimes the case that marginal staff are themselves suspicious of more senior managers in institutions but, as Hawkins and Winter (1997, p 40) go on to argue:

> The essential challenge ... [is] to move from isolated examples of
> successful practice to a state where new methods [have] deep roots in
> the institution. This means that the innovation must be incorporated in
> institutional systems and structures. Marginal activity must be brought
> into the mainstream of university or college life.

The most successful way of enabling marginality to develop into the mainstream is for those who have responsibility for staff who work on the margins to develop good communication systems. This approach enables institutions to use marginality to develop in new directions. As Smale (1996, p 82) argues: 'Research indicates that throughout the developmental period "home grown" innovations are usually implemented by linking and integrating the "new" with the "old", as opposed to substituting, transforming, or replacing the old with the new.'

Activities developed at the margins of organisations therefore provide an excellent seed ground for new 'home-grown' innovations. Valuing marginality and designing systems to use the experience gained from it requires commitment to the work at both strategic and operational levels. It also requires an appreciation of the challenges to institutional practice brought by staff who work at the margins. Working from the margins in this way is dynamic but it is not always comfortable. Helping staff acknowledge difficult insights from outsiders will take time but encouraging them to see potential benefit from changing practice will finally produce results, as Duke (1994, p 223) points out:

> Different means and modes of conveying leadership messages are heard and heeded in different ways within the institution.
>   The extent to which participants feel they are entering into a commitment to try something new voluntarily, or at any rate with some prospect of advancing their own (professional, departmental or individual) interests [is vital].

Marginal activity and the staff involved in marginality are an important resource for development and innovation in organisations. Much of the widening participation work done in colleges and universities involves staff in marginal projects working with external contacts and networks that will provide useful feedback for institutions. If marginality is to be beneficial to the development of organisations, project managers and their teams will need to gain access to the mainstream of institutions and senior managers should be more informed about the projects underway in their organisations. In the final section of this chapter, I take the discussion on learning within organisations further and show how reflection can facilitate the development of new and more appropriate practice for new learners.

The role of learning in the change management process

Change in education is perhaps best understood in relation to learning. In any learning situation, there is a period of discovering new ideas and practices, a period of trial as the learner practices and tries out their new skills and knowledge, and a period of reflection when the learning is evaluated. This cycle of learning is equally appropriate for a change-management process. New ideas need to be learnt and understood. They need to be tried out, and finally, they should be evaluated. At an individual level, reflection on process is a vital way that managers can develop solutions for future change. As Hawkins and Winter (1997, p 39) point out: 'The habit of reflection ... is the best guarantee of learning from past experience ... It can make the difference between acting as a victim of circumstance and choosing a proactive response.'

Despite the temptation to take the next step towards change, periods of quiet when colleagues can evaluate changes already taking place will prove more effective for development than simply responding to pressures for further change. When an organisation is undergoing significant change, staff should be encouraged to participate in evaluating the change. This not only facilitates the changes required, but it also helps managers and their teams interrogate the future direction of the organisation. This gives staff more ownership of the process, which Taylor (1995, p 71) suggests is crucial: 'the key to staff development in a climate of change is taking staff with you and ensure that they not only understand change and the reasons for it but that they also have a sense of ownership of the change process.'

Reflection contributes to an inclusive management approach that creates an engaged and committed staff group. Learning is an everyday activity in educational institutions, but learning between staff in educational organisations is, surprisingly, still in its infancy. It will need to become a more central focus for organisations if they are to meet the challenges facing the sector. Managers need the courage to lead change and also to create opportunities for reflection and learning from change to enable effective development for the future.

In this chapter, I have discussed the process of managing organisations and suggested new ways of managing in organisations that highlight partnerships between staff and students. However, it is increasingly clear that in order to support any form of widening participation in F and HE, partnerships beyond organisations with different groups are vital. The challenges that such working represents are draw out by Pratt *et al* (2000, p 86) when they say:

> In a single organisation, strategy serves to guide and give coherence to decisions and actions. In a whole system made up of many organisations there is just as much need for strategy but its form has to be different. The mechanism of accountability is different in a complex system – there is no one owner or boss who is responsible for its functioning and to whom people are accountable. Decisions are made in a variety of situations and need to be sensitive to individual circumstances.

In the next chapter, I take the discussion forward to examine how widening participation activities can be facilitated through such complex systems of partnership.

4 Made for each other? Collaboration, partnerships and power

In encouraging partnership arrangements in the provision of opportunities for learning, it is necessary to address the unequal power relations that currently exist between various stakeholders within the educational system as a whole. These relations must be managed in ways that ensure genuine forms of participation re-distribution and empowerment, particularly in favour of marginalised and excluded groups. This has significant implications for institutional structures, inter-professional relations and funding policies and procedures (Martin, 1999, p 101).

Terms such as partnership, collaboration and joint working are increasingly part of the vocabulary in F and HE and are often seen as pre-requisites for widening participation (Action on Access, 2001; DfEE, 1999b). Yet, seldom does the literature provide a critical engagement with the day-to-day practicalities of partnership working. Neither, as Martin points out above, are questions of power relations and participation between groups and organisations fully examined. This chapter explores some of the challenges that a collaborative approach to widening participation presents. It examines the process of partnership, the different levels at which partnership operates, and how power and partnership are intertwined.

Collaborative working has been a feature of much social care and health provision since the 1980s, and here I suggest that the roots of a partnership approach in education are to be found in these developments in social policy. Drawing on the lessons learned from health and social welfare and further and higher education partnerships, the chapter suggests that there is no one ideal partnership model, but rather different types of partnership for different purposes. I begin by examining what partnership means.

Defining partnership

Within current policy documents on widening participation and lifelong learning there are a range of assumptions, about the role of F and HE in challenging social exclusion, in 'spreading' knowledge wider and in working with others to achieve these ends. When developing a change agenda for FE, Kennedy (1997, p 13) argued that the government should 'create a national network of strategic partnerships to identify local need, stimulate demand, respond creatively and promote learning'. The Dearing Committee report on Higher Education (Dearing, 1997, recommendation 3) recommended that: 'With immediate effect, the bodies responsible for funding further and higher education in each part of the UK collaborate and fund – possible jointly fund – projects designed to address ... and to promote progression to higher education.' Later Dearing (1997, recommendation 85) also suggests partnerships to facilitate 'better information [for] students about higher education opportunities ... and to work together to improve timely dissemination of the information'. The government lifelong learning partnership initiative provides the commitment for Kennedy's and Dearing's recommendations. The remit document (DfEE, 1999b), which outlines the requirement to establish the partnerships, states (p 1): 'Partnership and collaboration are essential to achieving the government's goals for economic prosperity and social cohesion through regeneration, capacity building and community development.' Equally, the LSC (LSC, 2001, p 14) highlights in its draft corporate plan the need for partnership to achieve its aims for raising achievement and participation:

> The Learning and Skills Council cannot of course deliver major improvements alone. Everything we do, either nationally or locally, will need to be in partnership with a complex interlocking set of private and public agencies.

As well as policy makers, colleges and universities also highlight the importance of partnership. Watson and Taylor (1998, p 115) point out that many universities reflect a desire to work in partnership:

> Virtually all universities refer in their institutional plans to the need for good relations and partnerships with their local communities, although only 47% of traditional universities regard this as a high priority compared with 74% of new universities.

It is therefore possible to detect in policy and in educational establishments' mission statements many examples of a desire to see partnership embedded in practice. However, there are fewer accounts of how these partnerships work, or indeed, what exactly is meant by 'partnership'.

The word partnership is used in everyday conversation but the idea of what a partnership is varies according to context. There are many different types of partnerships, from personal relationships through to business and other professional groupings, such as legal firms and doctors' practices. This diversity suggests a need for greater clarity about the nature and purpose of the partnerships we wish to create.

In using a partnership approach to widen participation in education, an understanding of local need is required (DfEE, 1999b, p 7). It also demands a better understanding of the core processes of partnership so that the relationships developed between partners can be used more effectively and creatively. This understanding has been found to be lacking in some instances. For example, in evaluating provision in FE for adults with learning difficulties and disabilities, Tomlinson (1996 p 122) found that 'the processes involved in collaboration are not understood by all managers and are not evaluated rigorously'. In an attempt to support partnership arrangements between HE and FE, Action on Access produced a code of practice for partnerships. It suggests (2001, p 2) that:

> working in partnership requires particular skills. Instead of direction and control, the skills of negotiation and influence are important. Loose, time limited, coalitions of interest to share risks, resources and skills in pursuit of a shared goal replace more rigid solutions.

This style of approach is very different to many of the more structured approaches taken by F and HE institutions. In some cases, it may require the loss of authority, or the abandonment of particular structures to enable the partnership to flourish.

Within the field of social welfare and health, partnerships to support inclusion and 'community care' have been well established for nearly 20 years. During the 1980s, health and social welfare professionals were encouraged to develop joint plans to facilitate care provision for people who were moving out of institutions into local community settings. As well as conducting joint planning, health and social welfare organisations were encouraged to allocate their funding jointly. Community care planning included a range of stakeholders: local authority social services, health authorities and trusts, voluntary and private care providers and users of services. The aim of all this joint strategic planning was to enable previously excluded groups, such as people with learning difficulties or mental health difficulties, to live lives integrated within a local community. Many of the policy decisions at the time focused on a mixed economy of care with a greater emphasis on private and voluntary sector providers of services. Strategic planning was seen as a solution to avoid duplication and to ensure that services met the expressed needs of users.

While obviously there are differences between a widening participation education agenda and social care, the story of social care provision has strong echoes in education: the development of learning partnerships, the composition of the LSCs and the encouragement from funders to draw in different, and sometimes new, stakeholders in widening participation projects. It seems likely that government and policy makers have used many of the ideas from health and social welfare reforms of the 1980s and 1990s to formulate their plans for life-long learning and widening participation.

Research undertaken since the development of joint planning in health and social welfare indicates that these partnership were, essentially, about 'jointness', joint responsibility and accountability and sometimes joint activity (Poxton, 1996, p 10). The literature goes on to suggest that any partnership will need to contain three essential elements:

1. a mutual sense of purpose;
2. a joint agreement of future action; and
3. collaborative working.

This definition creates a useful starting point for evaluating the creation and development of partnerships to support widening participation in F and HE. However, these three aspects of partnership cannot be taken for granted as they proved to be difficult to achieve. Referring to social care partnerships, Wistow (1994, p 24) argues that 'it is universally recognised that joint working of all kinds has been an area of major disappointment and failure in the recent history of community care.' The experience from those more practised in partnership is not positive. The experience in FE suggests that working together is difficult. In Chapter 2, I argued that despite the growing emphasis on collaboration, competition is still part of the culture of F and HE. Rather than finding collaborative working easy, colleges have a tendency to wish to compete, as Kennedy (1997, p 3) found:

> Competition has been interpreted by some colleges as a spur to go it alone. Other colleges are seen as rivals for students rather than as potential collaborators with whom good practice and a strategic overview can be shared and developed.

She argues (1997, p 39) that there is little effective use of partnerships that already exist:

> Many of the key local stakeholders in post-16 education and training therefore meet repeatedly in different forums to discuss similar and linked issues. We are concerned that this flowering of consultation, partnership and inter-agency networking is often focused on single issue activities and masks the absence of any fully effective local strategic dimension in determining the character of and priorities for public investment in FE. The absence of a strategic dimension at local level is, in our view, a major weakness in the system which significantly reduces the potential for widening participation.

The Tomlinson Report (1996) also argued for a cultural change in the organisation of learning in colleges. He suggests that individual learners' needs should dictate educational provision, rather than learners being required to fit into an educational system already determined. He argues (1996, p 8) for collaboration between agencies and groups to create inclusiveness in learning: 'A further feature of an improved service will be extending collaboration with other services, especially health, social work, the LEAs, TECs and voluntary organisations.' However, he also goes on (p 122) to point out that collaboration has been difficult to achieve: 'Competition between colleges and schools, between neighbouring colleges and between colleges and other providers of post-school education and training is a major barrier to joint planning.'

Partnership in F and HE has proved illusive in many situations, often because of structural incentives to create a climate antithetical to collaboration. In other words, despite recognition that partnership is a 'good idea', there is little that has overcome its complexities or the difficulties in facilitating its success. Nevertheless, it is difficult to see how widening access and participation to F and HE can be achieved unless new partnerships between groups and organisations are made to work, and the next section examines what partnerships can offer widening participation.

Delivering 'widening participation' through partnership

The dominant argument for widening participation in F and HE focuses on an economic imperative to develop a more competitive workforce. The development of social cohesion or inclusion is an obvious precursor to the requirements of the economy. So far in the book I have also discussed the less powerful but equally valid discourse of the need for a social purpose model of learning (Field, 1998; Johnston, 1999; Stuart and Thomson, 1995; Taylor and Ward, 1986) which champions a belief in active citizenship for all community members. At the heart of this perspective lies an argument that access to knowledge empowers people, helping them to challenge decisions that are being made about their lives, thereby enabling the wider population to take more control of what they experience on a daily basis.

Whether the impetus for widening participation is economic strength, social cohesion or based on notions of social purpose, effective partnerships emerge as the logical solution to countering educational inequalities. If the purpose is developing a well-educated workforce who can withstand the current capitalist fashion for 'flexibility', then partnerships between employers, trade unions and education are essential to ensure that the education and training provided is relevant and that workers are given access to that training. Equally, if the widening participation agenda is to be more community focused, including not only people's work experience but also their whole lives and their potential contribution to wider society, a range of partnerships across professions, groups and communities becomes even more significant. The major reason for joint approaches to enable greater participation in F and HE has to be the recognition that 'no one profession should assume that it has all the answers or can meet all the needs' (Kneale, 1994, p 154). As well as partnerships with relevant groups and professionals to enable access to communities and individuals who have not as yet participated in continued learning, partnerships between educationalists and other groups in the community can be of value to communities. If links between different types of services and providers are not forged and joint planning is not facilitated, duplication, disorganisation and, possibly even worse, conflicting strategies will be the result.

Tomlinson, in his committee's extensive research on FE provision for people with learning difficulties and disabilities, found this problem all to often. He said (1996, p 124) that:

> the absence of good local networks and opportunities for collaborative planning meant that some colleges had difficulty in analysing local community requirements effectively, provision might be duplicated by different providers. Some groups of learners might not have provision made for them, it was difficult to track the students as they moved from

school to college and on to employment or further training and to ensure that they received the right services at the right time.

Partnerships are, therefore, also vital for community and business development. Effective and successful partnerships are two-way. This means that F and HE institutions will not only benefit by gaining access to potential new students, but all the partners in a project or strategic development should gain a deeper insight into different approaches to working with people who experience exclusion. Effective partnership can therefore create a climate of mutual understanding and a greater sharing of ideas often offering a fresh approach to activity.

When the Open University (OU) decided to develop a new programme of study with a range of partners in the field of learning disability studies, they included not only organisations such as Mencap but also People First, a national self-advocacy group run by and for people with learning difficulties. Reflecting on their initial perceptions of the partnership, the OU team reported:

> When we set out we thought of it as a one-way relationship, one in which the Open University had to bend over backwards to make it possible. We had not expected a two-way relationship when we began working together, it was only as our partnership developed that we realised how important sharing was (Walmsley, 1993, p 103).

The team found that the discipline of ensuring that meetings and activities were well planned and did not run on too long, that instructions were clear and direct and that differing perspectives were presented and debated meant that many of the work practices within the department changed for the better. In any work environment, we accept a number of 'taken-for-granted' practices, which need questioning and challenging if we are to develop. Working with others who have different practices can help us all challenge our prejudices and assumptions. As Watson and Taylor (1998, p 119) have argued:

> For community education to be successful it must arise as a genuine dialogue between the community and the university, and not be imposed by the university. It is not a question of the university offering its provision on a 'take-it-or-leave-it' basis, rather, the university must adapt and develop its provision to meet the needs of the community.

For the two-way nature of partnerships to be successful, educationalists should listen carefully to others and the partnerships should develop a shared agenda of value to the people that the projects are there to support.

Indeed, recent research on local community needs highlights that the central concern for people in deprived areas is not education or exclusion but issues that have relevance to their daily lives, as Quinn (2001, p 14) describes:

> Social inclusion as a concept has little meaning to individuals from disadvantaged communities ... in Raploch, a deprived part of Stirling, the main community issues to emerge from a recent survey were not social inclusion, but drugs, housing, planning and crime.

F and HE have not themselves been able to gain access to the communities and people who have had limited opportunity to participate in F and HE. While working directly in communities was a notable feature of FE during the 1970s and early 1980s, this approach had largely disappeared by the late 1990s, as Zera and Jupp (1983, p 3) highlight:

> Outreach work is still just about alive ... where tutors work the housing estates, knock on doors and talk to people about the possibilities. Perhaps for the future we can devise a mix of something more sophisticated but equally personal to make the connections. We need to engage the active involvement of an army of well-briefed outreach workers (health visitors, social workers, probation officers, youth workers, school teachers, personnel officers and others) to explain that it's worth keeping connected.

Further, Watson and Taylor (1998, p 119) argue that to facilitate widening participation the following partnerships are a minimum requirement:

> Almost all successful provision of community education has been organised as a partnership between the university and the LEA, further education college, voluntary body (tenants' association, unemployed centre, ethnic minority group etc.) trade union or some other similar body.

Widening participation across the sector will not succeed without partnership, but partnerships are difficult to maintain. Equally, partnerships can have a range of purposes and, in the next section, I suggest that part of the difficulty with partnership working is a lack of understanding that different partnerships require particular approaches to help them succeed.

Different partnerships for different purposes

In examining social care partnerships across the country, Pratt *et al* (2000) argue that partnerships should be fit for the purpose. Partnerships operate at different levels. In much of the education literature, the emphasis is on only one form of partnership, the strategic partnership. Strategic partnerships focus on long-term planning, usually drawing on partners who have influence and power in an area. There is almost a belief in strategic partnerships being the 'saving grace' of widening participation. Kennedy, Dearing and the Lifelong Learning Partnership initiative all focus on this level of partnership. While joint strategic planning may be vital to the success of a widening participation agenda, other levels of partnership within and between organisations and groups also require attention and support. In 1999 the Director of the Centre for Continuing Education at Central University expressed his concern with lifelong learning partnerships in this way:

> Lifelong learning partnerships are a form of partnership that focuses on strategic change, bringing together the economic agenda, and that is relatively new. So I can see that you need those mechanisms to do that but

I also think who is driving the agenda and how can the people who are on the ground effect it? That is the bit where I have question marks.

Partnerships can also operate at project or activity level. These will bring in different players who work more locally. Their partnerships will often be time-limited and will draw in people who have a specific interest in the activities planned for the project. Partnerships that are only based on senior management initiatives, even if they have been planned jointly, carry with them the seeds of failure if they do not address the implications for their staff and the potential students that they wish to attract. The experience of health and social welfare workers shows that if partnerships occur only at the strategic level, difficulties will arise in delivery (Arblaster *et al*, 1996; Wistow, 1994).

Strategic partnerships will bid for funds to establish specific projects based on evaluations of local needs. Project partnerships will usually include middle managers within organisations and their commitment and ownership of projects will be an important factor in developing success. They in turn will work with their teams to develop appropriate learning activities. This creates another level of potential partnership working, which will include links between development workers, tutors, potential students and their representatives; that is to say, partnerships need to be developed at three different levels:

- strategic planning;
- project development;
- operational activity.

Involving all levels of staff, a range of professionals and local people in this way presents a number of challenges for managers of widening participation projects, and implementation of this strategy will need to be planned according to the culture of organisations and groups involved. As Flude (1999, p 16) noted from his experience of working in rural partnerships:

> Strategic partnerships are intended to provide support of the development of widening participation strategies and lifelong learning. Those working at the grass roots, at the ends of these funding streams, will have to be pro-active and will have develop these working relationships.

The complexity of partnership working presents challenges for managers within organisations in terms of not only how they negotiate with other partners outside their organisation but also how they enable their staff to deliver on the ground. Partnership working requires the commitment and determination of staff at all levels across organisations. This requires a whole organisational cultural shift to encourage a more outward-looking approach to learning.

Adizes (1992), writing about working together in a business environments, explores the nature of the kind of teamwork required for staff to work in partnership. He says (p 221) that building these corporate and collaborative systems requires understanding and trust:

> When children make up games, the first thing they do is agree upon the rules. If someone breaks the rules, they stop playing and fight. Any interdependence in life is governed by rules. We just have to discover them.

> There is no functional interdependence without rules of conduct ... there is
> no teamwork without mutual respect and trust and there is no mutual
> respect and trust without adherence to mutually agreed upon rules of
> conduct.

In other words, it is vital to ensure that the partners discuss what they expect
from each other and how they hope to work together. This clarity will prevent
misunderstanding in the end and enable the development of trust because the
work of the partnership is clearly defined. To return to Pratt *et al*'s fit for
purpose definition they argue (2000, p 99) that:

> What seems to matter most is that there is clarity about the purpose of a
> partnership. We distinguish between ... co-ordination and co-evolution
> [partnership methods]. Each requires different behaviour [and I would
> argue, often different players] to achieve its ends and when these
> behaviours and purposes get muddled up then the frustration with
> partnership grows.

One of the major drivers for change in F and HE has been the funding council
incentives, such as collaborative bidding between organisations, to try to foster a
climate of 'partnership'. In examining a range of partnerships across Britain, Pratt
et al (2000) found that most of the strategic partnerships investigated emphasise
clarity of boundaries between partners as the most important factor for their
success. They suggest that this approach is designed to enable the allocation of
funds between institutions, as each partner is clear about what they can offer, and
funds are duly allocated in proportion to activity. They suggest also that this is the
sort of approach most favoured by government bodies, since each of the elements
of the partnership is easy to identify and accountability is clear. Pratt *et al* refer to
this type of arrangement as being a co-ordinated partnership. Many of the current
funded partnerships in further and higher education take a co-ordinated
approach. In Staffordshire, for example, a partnership has developed between
nine further education college principals, the local Local Education Authority
Directors, the Chief Executive Officer of the career service, the Vice Chancellors
of the local universities, the Open College Network director and the Training and
Enterprise Council. The Principal of Staffordshire College highlighted that:

> Formulating a bid for funding gave us the opportunity of concentrating on
> the best approach given the limited available resources ... Each link worker
> is managed by someone in a further education college, usually the Head of
> Community and Access who is sitting on the steering group representing
> the College. The model we were looking for was linkworkers drawn from
> the community being served. As such, this person understands the
> community culture, its network of contacts, how it operates and how it
> could be motivated into action. The linkworkers would help the colleges
> understand how to reach and widen participation in those focused wards.
> They could also network with other initiatives including Single
> Regeneration Budget (SRB) work, New Deal locality groups, Careers
> Services, and lifelong learning staff and therefore reinforce existing activity
> (Megson, 1999, p 41).

One of my interviewees, a senior manager at Capital City University, who had been involved in partnership working for over ten years, also highlighted the need for clarity and honesty between partners:

> Partnerships only work if you are quite open with your self-interests within that partnership. I now know the difference between partnerships; good partnerships, where people are open about what their interests are as well as some of the boundaries where they are not prepared to be partners. I think as long as it is transparent; there can not be any misunderstandings.
>
> So partnerships should not just be about signing up for the sake of getting a grant, as this approach will lead to conflict ... We need to try to say, 'this is what I can do', 'that is what you can do', 'this is what we can do together' and 'this is where we are not going to work together'. I think that is a very important step if we can define outputs that we can deliver. There is nothing worse than going into a partnership and then finding out that you cannot deliver (1999).

The other type of partnership mentioned by Pratt *et al* are those that evolve over time and that attempt to solve issues that do not as yet have clearly defined solutions – what are termed co-evolutionary partnerships. These partnership are usually based on relationships that have built over time and where a mutual sense of passion for the values of the partnership will carry participants forward, even if they are stepping into the unknown. These type of partnerships are often creative but are usually more difficult to fund and can create anxieties for managers because they are not always able to see the outcome of the effort which their staff invest. In reality, most partnerships go through different stages and may well have elements of either type of partnership, both co-ordinated and co-evolutionary, as Pratt *et al* (2000, p 99) acknowledge: 'Real partnerships include elements from several at any one time and are likely to move between them over the course of time.'

Having defined the scope of partnerships in the sector, it is important to realise that in complex working relationships, 'negotiating ... with community contacts, who are operating in a very different context to a university (or college) requires considerable diplomacy' (National Taskforce for Widening Participation, 2000, p 38). This is a wide range of people and will throw up potential conflicts between partners, and in the next section I examine some of the key issues which surface in the process of partnership development such as conflicting agendas and cultural diversity.

The process of partnership

When examining the experience of health and social welfare partnerships, differing agendas or conflicting aims were noted as problems in developing and sustaining joint working. Some of the literature highlights the problem by using the term 'collaboration'. Some theorists do not like the term but it does point up a significant problem with partnership working. Loxley (1996, p 1) notes: 'it carries implications of the enemy, of the other, to be regarded with some suspicion.'

Working collaboratively will present partners with clashes of culture and of different approaches as well as professional boundary issues, all of which need to be addressed properly if partnerships are to have a chance to succeed. As Pratt *et al* (2000, p 94) point out:

> Decisions need to be based on fitness for purpose rather than historical precedent or institutional power or habit ... As the public sector becomes increasingly deregulated, boundaries between agencies multiply. Since boundaries are frequently the site of failures of communication, understanding, respect and cooperation, it is not hard to see that the problem, and possibly the solution, lies in cross-boundary working.

In any management strategy, questions should be asked about who would be the most suitable members of a partnership to enable the project to succeed. Calman (1994, p 96) highlights the need to include 'a mix of skills and in so doing all members ... have to recognise the skills and expertise of others'. Partners must think beyond their own worlds and become involved in activities beyond their own working environment. This will provide them with a greater depth of knowledge about their communities and region and will enable them to be included in partnerships developed by other groups and agencies. In other words, using partnerships to widen participation in the F and HE sectors is not a swift option; it takes time to grow a presence, to mature links and to develop sufficient trust to enable people at whatever level to work together.

In entering any partnership, there are four main areas of partnership development work that need attention. These are: structures; systems; relationships; and interactions. These elements can be described as the living elements of a partnership. The structures are like the bones of the partnership providing a framework to enable participants to understand what they are working together to achieve. The systems are like the arteries, muscles and nervous systems, which communicate information and enable action. The relationships, rather like the senses of a living organism, enable the creature to attune itself to development and be able to take on change, and the interactions are like the distinguishing features which provide nuance and definition making the partnership, what it is and influencing its success or failure.

In analysing the process of partnerships for widening participation, managers need to consider a number of questions with common themes:

- Are there appropriate structures in place for the partnership to function?
- Are there communication and support systems that can sustain partnership work?
- Are there sufficient opportunities for partners to develop and build the relationships necessary for partnership?
- Are daily interactions between partners effectively facilitated and monitored to prevent misunderstanding and build trust?

Running through each of these four areas are a number of important issues, that any manager of widening participation must examine. These issues are power, difference and social inequalities, and professional boundaries. The rest of this chapter explores some of the dilemmas and challenges faced by managers, in supporting staff and as members of partnerships themselves, in tackling these issues.

The games that people play – powerful engagements

The strategy to widen participation in F and HE is based on a theoretical perspective that suggests that society is presently torn in two, separating those who are included in the processes of our society and those who are excluded. There is a belief that exclusion creates disempowered people and that inclusion provides greater choice and potential social capital (Schuller and Field, 1998). Partnerships developed to extend participation in further and higher education cannot ignore these dilemmas but must actively seek to resolve the tensions in the work.

Like partnership, power operates at different levels. Institutions reflect, and contribute to, the power differentials in society. They themselves are stratified in their ability to gain access to resources and voice within society. After Kennedy (1997), Schuller *et al* (1999) have pointed out that FE has been less powerful than HE, both in terms of resourcing but also in terms of influence. For many further education colleges, the experience of partnership with HE is that it is not a partnership at all, but rather 'higher education telling everyone else what to do' (Principal Northern City College, 1999). Equally, community colleges and independent adult education centres have similar stories about working with FE. Even in the education world itself, power is an important and difficult component of partnership.

Competition between institutions has already been highlighted in the relevant research as a major barrier to partnership in education (Kennedy, 1997; Tomlinson, 1996; Watson and Taylor, 1998). It is not an easy problem to resolve as resources are limited. As is also highlighted in health and social welfare partnerships, Hudson (1987, p 175) points out:

> from an agency's viewpoint, collaborative activity raises two main difficulties. First, it loses some of its freedom to act independently, when it would prefer to maintain control over its domain and affairs. Second it must invest scarce resources and energy in developing and maintaining relationships with other organisations, when the potential returns on the investment are often unclear or intangible.

Many of these problems are further exacerbated when broader partnerships are developed to include others such as community and voluntary sector groups. At the heart of all these difficulties lies a taken-for-granted value judgement that access to financial resources should automatically determine the leadership style of a partnership. This is a deeply ingrained belief. For example, Lifelong Learning Partnerships were given the following remit: 'in each case partners will need to identify a lead body to be accountable for partnership funding and to take a convening role' (1999, p 4). Connecting a lead body for funding with convening in the same sentence does suggest to many that these roles will be interchangeable even if the document does not prescribe this. The spirit of the remit document is one of joint ownership of the partnership as demonstrated by the range of potential partners that the document advocates. However, even here there are entrenched problematic beliefs that have created difficulties in partnerships at the outset. For example, creating a two-tier structure which identifies 'essential' partners on the one hand and 'optional' partners on the other produced an outcry from many potential partners creating unnecessary power differentials between core and periphery 'members'. If partnerships are to learn the lessons of past experience, such as the joint planning schemes of health and social welfare, then some notion of shared accountability and shared control is vital to enable trust between partners.

In working with groups of rural partnerships to widen participation, Flude (1999, p 17) points out that creating a progressive framework of activities 'allows partners to identify a part of the process on which they can focus so they can play a role which they find manageable'.

Resources, status and difference

The power/resource map of a partnership should begin with an initial recognition of suitable partners, creating equality between them. In work to widen participation, the question of the right partners is key. A mix of skills and knowledge fit for the purpose of the partnership is vital. Partners should be seen to have equal status and authority in the partnership no matter what their position is outside the partnership.

As well as status and authority issues, access to resources are key areas of contention for partnerships. Who controls the finances is seen to be the most significant factor in partnership working. Yet, traditional conceptions of resource power determining activity has consistently created failure. Focusing on financial resource power misses the purpose of these partnerships. In work to support widening access and participation, the most significant factor should be how to ensure under-represented groups become involved in learning. Any successful partnership that has inclusion or active citizenship as its goal will recognise that there are other types of resource power apart from financial resources relevant to this type of work. In particular, such partnerships will need the resources inherent in knowledge of a community, the understanding of local history and an experiential appreciation of particular people's realities. Rather than trying to pretend that differences do not exist between partners, differences should be highlighted and then recognised and used as powerful resources to enable success. As Pratt et al (2000, p 35) point out:

> The presence of many perspectives is an essential resource. By contrast the search for one correct perspective reduces the capacity to adapt. The challenge of whole-system working is to find processes which exploit different ways of seeing things and making them available for use.

The resource power of partners required to widen participation will therefore include not only funding but appropriate infrastructure such as facilities used by local people, staff who are accessible and appropriately trained as well as a range of knowledge resources including local understandings, appropriate language skills, theoretical and analytical skills and the ability to ensure continued knowledge development within the partnership. Partners who are able to bring with them local credibility and trust, and skills and experience in working collaboratively, will also enable partnerships to succeed.

Mapping the different resource power available to a partnership will help shed light on gaps in the team and helps the participants to identify what strengths the group can exploit. Strategic partnerships will be able to plan more effectively if they have members who can provide appropriate local knowledge, understanding and credibility, project partnerships will be able to develop appropriate delivery strategies, and activity partnerships will have the framework of support and appropriate resources in staff and facilities to ensure delivery of activities meets their targets. At the start of any partnership, therefore, mapping resources and being clear about contributions will help to dissipate traditional power differentials that exist outside the bounds of the partnership.

Socially constructed power differentials do not only occur at this organisational level. The different organisations or groups within a partnership will be represented by individuals who bring with them a range of other socially defined roles. Social divisions in our society are commonly drawn in terms of gender, race and ethnicity, class and disability. Theorists (Thompson, 1988, Ward and Taylor, 1986) have noted that social divisions create inequalities in the classroom. Equally social divisions can reverberate inequalities between members of a partnership. Like the different experience that organisations bring to a partnership, which should be recognised and valued as appropriately contributing to a widening participation agenda, so too difference between partner members should be valued. If these differences are ignored then inequalities will flourish, threatening the success of the partnership. As G Coleman notes (1991, p 13) in discussing gender inequalities in team working:

> It is the informal ... which needs to be addressed if their gender
> implications are to be rendered meaningful. The informal is the backcloth
> against which the formal is played out, and it includes the personal and
> private arenas.

Paying attention to the informal is equally important in partnership work as it is in the informal that taken-for-granted discriminations are most evident. The experience and perspective of first hand social inequality will prove vital to facilitate sensitive delivery of appropriate provision and relevant design of strategy and project outcomes.

The role for managers of staff involved in partnerships is to ensure that they and their staff are both sensitive and aware of the value of difference and that the individuals whom they support are secure and comfortable within their roles in partnerships. The principal of Northern City College highlights the need for staff from minority ethnic communities to have support and redress mechanisms in their work environment as managers cannot control experiences that staff may have in wider partnerships. He sees his role as often being one of acting as an advocate for staff by challenging prejudice where it occurs.

In the Access and Guidance Unit of Yorkshire University, the manager provides support and training for her staff who are developing activities in working class communities. She says, 'they need to appreciate the culture of the communities, to understand and appreciate the language. It is only though doing this that the partnerships work' (Access and Guidance Co-ordinator, 1999).

In the development of partnerships, power plays a significant role. However, if partners at various levels acknowledge the issues raised by power and social inequalities explicitly in the early stages of a partnership, and mechanisms for support and development are planned and built into the partnership, this major stumbling block to successful joint working can be avoided. The significance of the role of individuals themselves to make the difference in creating a collaborative ethos cannot be underplayed. As Hornby (1993, p 174) notes from her research with development workers, 'in the end it comes back to each individual and their capacity to take risks with their self image'. The manager's role is to create the safety for staff to feel that they can experiment with role boundaries because they have sufficient support to develop their work in the partnership. The next section will explore another area that can cause difficulties in creating success, that of boundaries and professional status.

Treading on others' toes – partnerships and boundaries

Within the literature on widening participation there is an expectation that partnerships will consist of a range of organisations and people who provide specific expertise to enable a greater variety of people to become learners. This means that in the first instance in any partnership, people become members with the expectation that they are taking on a specific role, which has been pre-defined by their expertise. Educationalists, for example, would see their involvement in a partnership being related to their expertise in developing learning. Their primary allegiance and major world view is likely to be to, and of, education and they may well have an expectation that they will be the lead spokesperson on any learning issue in the partnership. Equally, in a partnership between a FE college and a university, it is likely that the representative from the university will expect the further education college representative to focus on pre-university entry work and the university to focus on university level work. However, in entering a partnership these job role divisions may not always be appropriate. In defining the purpose of the partnerships, all members of the group need to have some ownership of that purpose. The aims of the partnership should be mutually agreed and responsibility and commitment to secure those aims should be shared among all the partners. This means that while specific professional expertise must be utilised, the partnership must define for itself the most appropriate use of its members. In partnership work, at any level, the boundaries of job role which partners bring with them to the partnership will often be blurred and the sharing of expertise may not be fully apparent at the beginning of the arrangement.

In discussing the issues for health and social welfare professionals, Rawson (1994, p 39) points out that 'interprofessionalism challenges professionals to re-think their occupational purpose and to discover the most effective means of practice.' A good example of this approach is highlighted in one activity-based partnership in a coastal town in the south of England. The partners included a housing association, a local university, the Health Authority, Playlink, a young people's organisation and the tenants' association. In planning one activity the local housing association in conjunction with the health authority took the lead in providing a series of evenings on 'healthy homes'. These sessions provided information on heating, safety in the home, smoke detectors and crime preven-tion. The local community development worker from the university in the partnership had to re-think her role in the partnership as 'the' educationalist in the group, having to play a supportive role in this activity. She realised that 'the aim of the partnership was to develop the residents on the estate's ability to take more active control of their lives' and that this aim 'could be facilitated through different means' (Community Development Worker, 1999).

The boundaries of a job role have to be more fluid when taking on partici-pation in a partnership and new partnership roles will emerge. As management theorist Feyerabend (1975, p 20) argued, 'there should be a plea for a light touch of anarchy'. A degree of flexibility, at least, will enable greater creativity in part-nership work. Kneale (1994, p 152) pointed out in relation to community care provision that partnerships will not operate with traditional organisational cultures: 'collaboration implies a flattened hierarchy; a coming together to provide a service which may imply that the leadership within a team may shift according to the situation.'

This suggests that partnership working will influence the management style of institutions involved in the partnership. Partnership, like networking, is not organised through hierarchical line management responsibilities. It should be based on mutual responsibility and accountability. The difficulty for individual members of partnerships who may be employed within organisations that have clear reporting lines is that they will be expected to behave in the partnership as a colleague among equals yet in their work environment as a member of staff responsible to a manager.

For staff, this can create tensions in their own workplace as colleagues and managers may not understand that partnerships develop their own ethos and culture. Divided loyalties between their work for the partnership and their insti-tutional role have been a common experience for health and social welfare professionals (Rawson, 1994). In partnership working, members will focus on the set aims of the partnership, not the aims of the college or university. Managers need to be aware that their staff will have two agendas that they will need to fulfil, their own institution's agenda as well as the partnership's.

Within some areas of health and social welfare, the difficulties of partner-ship working have been resolved by developing new services, so-called 'seamless services'. Funded by a range of groups, these partnerships operate without the original organisation's control. Rawson (1994, p 46) pins down the central principle of seamlessness by noting that 'the concept of [a] seamless ... arrangement between professionals ... suggests the dissolution of boundaries'. These partnerships have taken on a life of their own. This approach could suggest a possible future for some aspects of educational activity that is jointly planned and funded. However, managers and staff involved in any partnerships should realise that allowing some flexibility to act within the partnership is vital. At the same time, ensuring good lines of communication between staff involved in partnerships will prevent misunderstandings and establish the limits of flexibility available. As Hornby (1993, p 167) points out, in collaborative working 'it is necessary to build mutual trust through open communication and the discussion of difficulties.'

As there are different interpretations of widening participation, from more conventional massification through to more radical versions that hope to engage new learners in the transformation of education itself, so too different partnerships will provide opportunities for widening access and participation. At its most radical, partnership working suggests a redefinition of professions and at least the re-negotiation of relationships and organisational cultures. Educationalists need to engage critically with these cultural shifts and explore what can be learnt from them. Working with 'others' in this way suggests challenges to educational institutions' ownership of knowledge. It draws out the range of different ways of understanding and experiencing daily life. If partnerships include the experience of socially excluded people, it will not always be a comfortable experience for professionals but it may be a necessary one. If widening participation is about including a wider range of people in 'what is', then co-operative and co-ordinated partnerships will produce results.

The agenda of social inclusion is multifaceted and is not necessarily radical in its intentions, and as I pointed out in Chapter 3, any manager needs to be very clear about their, and their institution's, position in this debate. Partnership working is not the solution to every problem but it is possible to use it to help education establishments explore different approaches to similar difficulties. It clearly offers a series of challenges for organisations participating in partnership work, but, if greater clarity of purpose can be achieved at an early stage of development, the rewards can be significant. The following three chapters examine how managers in a number of institutions have grappled with the management of change and partnership issues to develop their widening participation agenda.

5 The Cinderella service – institutional case studies from further education

In the classic Fairytale *Cinderella* the heroine works hard to enable her stepsisters to go to the ball while she sits in rags alone in the kitchen. It takes the transformation by her Fairy Godmother not only to get her to the ball but also to enable her to show how beautiful she is. Further education has been called the Cinderella service because of the need for its transformation and the recognition that FE as a sector has been underfunded. The 'magic' that is required to transform the service, however, is not only about funding. FE in Britain has always been seen as a part of successive governments' strategies to train young people for work in trade and industry. Its sister service, adult education (AE) had a more nebulous mission, providing both general-interest learning opportunities as well as more focused second-chance learning. However, by the late 1990s, 'adults were the clear majority of the FE college population' (Field, 2000, p 41). As a sector, therefore, F and AE have found themselves shifting significantly according to changing perspectives. Funding to undertake this work has varied according to the priorities of particular politics. The 1992 Further and Higher Education Act, which constructed FE colleges as public limited companies, not only developed an environment of capitalist competition between colleges but also changed many colleges' relationship to their communities. For many colleges, in a bid to balance their budgets and to attract more lucrative funding, their locality became less important when deciding on their educational offer. Many colleges retreated into their larger buildings, moving out of community venues to maximise their funds. Increasingly, FE colleges began to court overseas students who brought valuable funds with them. At the same time, the governance of colleges was increasingly moved towards business leaders rather than public service. This environment did not encourage the disaffected learner from taking on further study and, even in some cases, colleges avoided their local communities because such students were viewed as a liability.

The Kennedy report of 1997 suggested a radical revision of the competitive environment and stated, 'The key priority for public funding in post-16 learning must be to widen participation' (p 43). This change suggested a shift in ethos and practice, as Kennedy herself (p 83) acknowledged:

> Many of the successful schemes to attract people to education and training involve partnerships and collaboration. Partnerships can strengthen and support individual innovations for the benefit of the wider community.

FE was having to re-invent itself again. For those who had wholeheartedly embraced the notion of competitive engagement, cultural transformations within colleges were required. The Learning and Skills Council (LSC), which now funds FE, emphasises that widening participation is the central focus for the sector. Its mission is to 'raise participation and attainment through high-quality education and training' (LSC, 2001). Nevertheless, throughout the years of the Further Education Funding Council (FEFC) regime, there were examples in some colleges where community learning continued and projects to widen participation had developed despite the funding council's emphasis on competitive engagement. In her research for *Learning Works* (1997), Kennedy found that 'there is much existing and innovative practice throughout post-16 learning' (p 79).

This chapter discusses three case studies from colleges that have developed widening participation strategies, some of which maintained their community focus during the early 1990s and others which have shifted their focus more recently towards greater community involvement. Each of the examples has taken a different approach to their engagement with widening participation issues. One college particularly emphasised the importance of relationship building outside the college, using an outreach approach. Another was more concerned with the structures that would enable widening participation to transform the whole college, and a third college changed the systems within the institution to develop a more inclusive college, emphasising the students' need for progression.

Each college was involved in a variety of partnerships. The cultural environment of these different colleges affected the preferred approach to partnership. In one college where relationship building was the key feature of the management style, the principal felt comfortable with partnerships that were less task-orientated and more fluid. In another college where structures were more clearly articulated, the principal and her colleagues saw their successful partnerships being underpinned by clarity between the partners where boundaries were defined and activities shared out appropriately between partners. I am not suggesting that any of these colleges have reached some sort of widening participation gold standard. On the contrary, each example has approached the participation debate differently. Rather, I provide here some examples of real-life engagement with the question of participation. In some cases, inclusion is emphasised, in others an active participation model is being developed. The chapter therefore offers some suggestions for strategies to manage the process of change that is required to involve a greater diversity of learners in FE.

I discuss each college separately and provide the context of the college, its location, student numbers, budget, and so on. For each case study, I have focused on a specific element of the strategy of the college to widen participation. This provides a range of different approaches related to specific needs in different contexts. These three elements provide a loose agenda for managers of widening participation in colleges, which can be used to examine their own practice. These are:

- strategy and structures;
- issues of staffing, local need and equal opportunities; and
- innovative and creative ways of working to enable development.

Many people have argued that further education is managerially based on what Pritchard (2000, p 18) calls 'an aggressive ... masculinity'. Nevertheless, it is possible to find managerial approaches that create 'moments, spaces and gaps [which] exist between those practices demanded by managerial discourses' (Pritchard, 2000, p 19). It is these spaces that I wish to explore through my case studies. The managers I interviewed came from a variety of backgrounds, none of which reflected the conventional 'white, male middle-class' model. I do not hold that this automatically implies that their approach is better, but these managers argued that their situation was informed and determined by what could be called their 'otherness'. I discuss this point further in Chapter 7 but now turn to the first of the three FE case studies.

Local community provision – the case of Northern City College

Based in the heart of a large northern city, this college enrols in the region of 20,000 students each year. It has a staffing base of 924 lecturing and support staff and offers courses in 10 faculty areas, including a large provision in the performing arts. Its income, slightly exceeded by its expenditure, is in the region of £31million. Despite the small deficit, the college is doing well, developing new facilities and new partnerships with employers. One partnership with three large employers in the city has resulted in resources and work placements for students. The companies equipped a dedicated 'real-life office' where students could apply skills in a safe but realistic work environment. The companies also agreed to upgrade the equipment every five years providing a long-term partnership, in which all parties benefit.

Northern City College was highly commended in its inspection in 1997 for its extensive community links built over many years, and it is this area of work that I focus on here. For many colleges the 1992 F and HE Act signalled a major change in their relationship to their local communities. As Pritchard (2000, p 9) states: 'The narrow utilitarianism of the new FE ... [is] at the expense of a broad educational programme relevant to the local communities in which colleges operate.'

However, in Northern City College, the Principal, who arrived in 1991, took a very different view. Coming from the local area himself and, at the time, being one of the few black managers in further education, he was concerned to ensure that local people had appropriate access to learning. He told me:

> Over the years, we have always worked towards widening participation, and over the years we stuck to it.

MS: So, although colleges left, right and centre were – in the early nineties – pulling out of community work, you stayed with it?

We stuck with it and we saved it. Let me give you an example. In the mid 90s, an officer from the FEFC who was visiting said to me 'No wonder you are in financial difficulties, you have too many crèches and you don't have the money to run them', and I just said students want and need them and I wouldn't take any notice and now, all of a sudden, the people who were telling me stop this work are now coming and saying 'you're flavour of the month'. We believe in it not because some one's told us to do it. The government's agenda and the funder's agenda is now our agenda but we've not changed, we have the same agenda and we stick with it. Because in a place like this you've got to stick to it (1999).

In the college's strategic plan, the importance of equal opportunities is strongly represented. It is one of four main aims for the college. Their target student population is disadvantaged young people, unemployed adults and black and minority ethnic young people and adults. The college is actively involved in the city, developing a wide range of partnerships over the years, leading to its City of Learning initiative. The Principal told me about how they approached widening participation at the college.

MS: So, widening participation is about taking down the barriers, the things that stop people being taken away like providing crèches, like providing free courses ...?

Principal: Yes, but not only that.

Do you have people who work in communities? How do you handle that so-called 'outreach' thing?

We have a system where, for some time now, we have what we call drop-in study centres. We call them DISCs. While we have been closing our bigger buildings, we have been increasing our small buildings. They are all around in the community. We do a whole range of programmes in the community, fresh start, basic skills, and others ... Our adult basic education (ABE) programme is delivered through the DISCs. There are seven DISCs in college centres and two established in local libraries and four in community centres and two in community flats. The thing is that people have criticised drop-in work because people in the community do just that, they drop in and the staff can't control that. That's what's good about them though, we can't control it. The community can, they use the resources as they want to, not as we tell them to.

So even though you have lost buildings, the loss of buildings was to focus more directly on smaller more community focused work?

Yeah, we needed to focus more outside and so we worked with the community to provide these DISCs and the way it operates is that each of the poorest areas in the city has a partnership. There are nine city partnerships, and they are a mixture of groups and they are usually chaired by the city council. They include community leaders, the business sector and the public sector. Their main focus is to work to get money for their area to respond to the needs identified. The college has a manager on every partnership. I'm on one of them, too. There is a partnership board and some committees at city level and through these groups the community works out how it can get what it wants (1999).

Being involved over many years and remaining within local neighbourhoods enabled the college staff to develop solid relationships with local people and meant that when new initiatives came along the college was an obvious partner for people in the communities. Equally, the college would automatically turn to its community links to develop new partnerships and to plan its future work in the area. This is a clear example of co-evolving where relationships are at the heart of the ability to develop new and unexplored areas of joint working, because there is a high degree of trust already in existence. The college needed to be part of a range of local partnerships that discussed all the needs of the area, not just education. It was only in this context that the college was able to understand how educational provision could contribute to development, and not simply be add-on provision.

The Principal diversified his funding in order to continue his work in his own local area. Additional funding streams, especially from Europe, had been crucial to enable development particularly for the DISCs and other local community work, because the previous funding council had not funded such 'risky' and high-cost work.

In partnership with the Federation of Tenants Associations and supported by an ESF grant, the college developed resource facilities at the Federation's premises and on local housing estates. These resource centres provide flexible learning programmes, which enable local tenants to develop greater control of their own environment. Each of these examples grew out of partnerships developed over time where local planning became a joint activity. College managers were part of a team of people from different agencies and communities who worked together to support their area. I explored this long-term approach to partnership and relationship-building further with the Principal.

> MS: *What I find really interesting is that at the time when most colleges funded by FEFC withdrew into their big buildings and withdrew from the community, you got rid of your big buildings and worked in the community more. You were working in partnership more when other colleges set out to compete and you have been doing everything that they are now saying everyone is supposed to do.*

Principal: We're into partnerships in a serious way here. Don't get me wrong it can be a complete pain. You don't always see results and I have to admit that I sometimes question if the work is a good use of staff time. The community doesn't always see the college as a friend, they sometimes see us as a predator. You do get frustrated but you have to do it, we can't do everything and we don't know everything. That is why partnership is vital. You have to develop your relationships with people, learn to trust each other and listen for those moments when new ideas grow. Listening to what the community wants is the most important thing ... At incorporation, we retained our local political contacts. We kept local councillors on our board of governors and we have tried to stay close to them. We're the same people so we can work together. Our staff are good. Their relations with the communities are solid (1999).

When calls for a dedicated new arts centre were made in the late 1990s, the principal brought together a range of partners with whom the college had already worked and identified different funding possibilities to make the project happen. The new centre was opened in 1998 and its use and engagement with local people remains fluid and open. The Principal told me:

This centre is within a stone's throw from where the riots were and ... we open this building up to the community, so as well as students there are lots of black community groups who use it and do their own thing, so it might be a black dance company or whatever. We are trying to build this centre so that it is welcoming to local people so they can use the space. We charge the people who can afford to pay. We can get other community groups in and that is the way we build our relations with the local community, but I think people come in by different routes, people come in their own way ...

The issue of racial equality is of enormous importance in this city and the Principal has worked hard to develop appropriate equality strategies. He was very conscious of how important it was to attract the right staff to work with communities in the city. I asked him how this approach worked:

MS: *You've had all this experience of partnership work, you've put different members of staff into all these partnerships, obviously because not one member of staff can or should do it all, so how do you decide who does it and how do they feed back what's going on?*

Principal: We decide between each other, the senior management team ... we make sure all the senior people are on a partnership. I think it is that important. We pick people according to the needs of the community ... because not all staff are user friendly and that chemistry must be right. It is about credibility and trust. In our management meetings, we feed back what's going on. We have a sort of meeting of all reps on partnerships that highlights issues that have come forward and they are given guidance on issues they need to be aware of and need to pick up on, so there are those kinds of support meetings ... I sit on the partnership from my old area. It's largely a black neighbourhood, but if a white member of staff were to do it, it has got to be someone that the community is going to accept. We have an excellent woman working on the ground in ABE in that neighbourhood. She's been able to establish herself there. You have to be very careful that communities are happy with who is working there (1999).

The Principal recognised the need to be credible over time in communities and that feedback from community partnerships was crucial if mistakes were to be avoided. As he pointed out, sometimes the communities in the city did not see the college as a friend and to avoid misunderstandings good communication between staff as well as identifying the right staff to work in communities was vital. The Principal was also concerned about support for his staff. The college had a significant number of black lecturing and support staff and I asked him about how he supported his staff in the college, many of whom, like himself, came from the local area:

> Principal: The thing is, with black staff what I do really is ... give people the benefit of my experience by sharing with them. I had the same issues that they face and they need to adapt to deal with the situation that they face. I think that for black managers it's very, very difficult; the expectations on you are ridiculous. For me now, it's less so. I'm the principal and even before when you and I worked together, it was less so. I'm the boss, and there's certain sort of kudos that you have ...

> *MS Yes, your role gives you authority.*

> That's right, so it's less difficult, but when you're in middle management ... you have to manage effectively. It's sad to say, but for every white manager who's supportive, there are two who are in your face, checking how you do things and wanting to see if you do things properly, so black staff, managers, have got those kind of pressures and so it's really trying to reassure people about how they can deal with those pressures. The main thing is that the students depend on you and that has to come first, no matter who you are. You have to do the job properly and then we can sort it out and people need to be reassured that that's the way you operate and keep to those things. I think there are always times, of course, when people need support in how to deal with situations. I always try and advise black staff from my own experience. All staff have to have the confidence to confront issues and, as I say, in the college we periodically have sessions on equal opportunities issues as well as people saying what do I do about this and raise matters informally. It's fairly standard and everyday here, so that's it really, openness and no nonsense (1999).

The Principal argued that engaging with diversity and understanding difference had helped the college grow and develop. He told me that working in communities taught him and his colleagues about what education should be doing and, over the years, this had helped the college seek out other funds and develop new programmes. He believed that widening participation could not happen without the partnerships that they had developed. The Principal was not unrealistic. He acknowledged the work was difficult and was sometimes problematic but it was the only way that they could deliver what he and his colleagues believed they were there to do. During my research at Northern City College, what came across strongly was the importance placed on relationship building, within the college, but particularly between the college and the communities in the city. The college was outward looking, drawing its strength from the links that it had developed with community leaders and others in the city. Getting to know people and building trust were the key messages that lay at the heart of their strategy for enabling widening participation. As I left the college, the Principal walked me to the station. I was struck by the number of conversations he had with people on the streets. Some were informal and chatty while others were focused on business. I commented that he seemed to know everyone around. He laughed and said:

> I organised that for you, stage-managed the city! No really, people stay here, it's their city and when you've been around as long as I have you do get to know people. I've done some really good deals for new provision through informal chats. You just have to be interested and alive to possibilities (1999).

The culture of Northern City College was, and is, rooted in the permeability between the institution and the city. The Principal recognised that any encounter could be an opportunity. The college had developed its infrastructure significantly to make this level of engagement possible. The next college I visited had to take a different approach to developing its widening participation strategy, focusing on the need to transform the college itself.

Seaside College – using strategy and re-organisation to establish a culture for widening participation

Seaside College was in a very different position to Northern City College when the new principal arrived in 1998. The college was smaller than Northern City. It had a budget of £13million with around 15,000 students each year. There were 350 full-time teaching and administrative staff and 400 part-time staff. Focusing heavily on FE, with a small HE provision in partnership with a new university, it offered courses across the range of FE including caring services, computing and engineering. It could be described as a traditional FE college, largely based on two main sites in a medium-sized seaside town. The town lies on the south coast in the heart of the southern coastal deprivation belt. More than 80 per cent of local residents in social housing are in receipt of public benefits and unemployment has remained high despite an overall robust economy in the South East of England. Historically, the college had developed strong links with industrial employers and had not really addressed issues of widening participation until the new principal was recruited. Coming from a college in the West Country where she had increased the participation rates of local people in her college by nearly 30 per cent, she was committed to widening participation and realised that her new college needed considerable change if the widening participation agenda was to be delivered. When a new manager takes up post it is usual for them to engage in development work for a period of time. In this college, there had been a feeling that something new needed to happen and the trigger for that change was a new principal. As Smale (1996, p 80) puts it: 'It is the case that crises, or shocks trigger concentrated efforts to progress an innovation ...

These shocks may come from internal or external sources to the organisation.'

The Principal began by telling me her concerns about how widening participation is sometimes interpreted:

> I think there is a danger that education is seen as a panacea, that it is going to change everyone's life, that everyone wants it, but some don't. Some may say, 'No thank you, I'd rather go to the pub'. I think we mustn't make that assumption that everyone will want it or that it's right for everybody, and we certainly mustn't make the assumption that it will have an equal effect on everyone.
>
> There will be many reasons why people may not want to study. They may not be ready for it, but at least we need to do things in a different way and show that we are accessible to people. In other words, rather than the college saying 'this is what we have to offer – come and get it', we talk about how we can interest people, at the time and place that they want, with the support they need. We need to get that right.
>
> That leads to strategic planning which will include all the things that you do ... the way you market, the way you get out there, how you organise your partnerships and the curriculum ... We know we have good quality here, but we need to be asking ourselves all the time is this the best we can offer? ... and are we doing it in the right way so that more people can access it and become involved. I think we can do that at the strategic level and then at the operational level involving all staff, and this internal thinking helps maximise the development of our work (2000).

A whole-college approach to change management for widening participation to enable greater access for those who want to participate lay at the heart of the change that the Principal felt was required. In his review of inclusive learning, Tomlinson (1996, p 6) found this kind of strategic thinking sadly lacking in most college planning: 'Work seldom features in college wide systems, or strategic planning, quality assurance or data collection and analysis.'

I asked the principal to take me through the stages of development she saw necessary to transform the college:

> Okay let's stay with strategy. You think 'what is the organisation trying to achieve?', and we have agreed that it is widening participation. Now, how does it do that? I think we have to have a structure that facilitates widening participation ... couldn't just be any structure, it needs to be designed around the principles of widening participation. We need to get everyone signed up to that and constantly talk about it at corporation level and get it [widening participation and the structure] high on the governors' agenda.
>
> The next stage was examining the senior posts in the college. For this project to work, we felt we needed a key senior management post that oversaw the work, so we created a Director of Access and Student Services and right at the heart of that job is managing central student services and driving the college's widening participation agenda.

Next, we recruit the right person to do that, so you look at the skills required ... I think that is really important because there is going to be a whole raft of other problems and whoever is appointed needs the tools to be able to keep going when things get tough.

Now once you have your commitment and your governors' commitment and you get the right person to oversee the process, you need to support them to achieve the vision by giving them the right team. I believe we have made an excellent appointment. She has all the track record and certainly has all the value systems in place. We have a pretty good team now. We have more posts dedicated to guidance, to helping students, to tracking them, and those post holders are being developed and were selected to be customer friendly, so they are able to assist people into the right programmes.

We then looked at the physical space for access and decided we needed a whole new area for student services which is much more accessible, more open, more friendly. Then there will be central admissions so there are fewer places people have to go, less paperwork to complete to make the whole process easier for students and to ensure that everyone gets the right support, advice and help (2000).

The Principal recognised that implementing change on this scale required primarily the support of the governors. She told me she 'worked really hard on them' (2000). Clearly, any manager in this position needs to know they will have the backing of their governance structure, especially in times of change. The Principal, here, told me that the change process had not always been smooth. She said:

It was very hard for some people because it hits at the very basics, like job security and personal fulfilment, enjoying coming to work. Change does that. It makes people less secure. I try to operate a very participatory style but some things I know I have had to do autocratically. Culture change sometimes requires that determined push. I think we have a way to go to being entirely student-focused here. In most education contexts, the idea of 'I'm here, they come to me, I teach them and they learn' is still a major part of the system but for a widening participation agenda to work that has to change, and sometimes it needs that extra push on things. I needed all the help I could get. You can't do this alone and I needed to know the governors supported me (2000).

She also placed great emphasis on the personality and experience of her Director of Access and Student Services. The role of individuals was seen to be crucial to many of the managers I interviewed. Being able to work with colleagues in the institution and having the right networking skills to work beyond the institution requires a particular set of abilities. It was instructive how much emphasis was placed on these abilities by my interviewees. Having set in place a more welcoming environment, the next task was to look at the range of barriers that new students face in taking up study. The Director of Access and Student Services, the Principal's new appointee told me:

> In the past, it seemed that the college was making it more difficult for students so you need to remove those barriers. We are trying to improve our childcare facilities, despite the bureaucracy and regulations with the crèche. We are trying to make that as friendly as we can. We have been working on the admissions processes to make those more user friendly. For me, the crucial bit is looking at our routes in and through learning, so new students can start with us or start somewhere else and easily follow through. Progression is very important; it is not just about access. But at the college, we also need to develop projects that encourage new people to come into education. We are now working in the local community. The college didn't used to do that, can you believe it? Once new students have had a go at learning in their own area, they build up the confidence to come to the bigger buildings. We have just run a course to give women a chance to come in and do a small taster programme which will lead to them becoming supporters of other members of their community who might like to try a course, or whatever, sort of learning advocates (2000).

The college is nearly 60 miles away from the nearest university and the Principal felt that part of the widening participation mission of the college should be to provide locally accessible higher education. However, she felt she would rather develop this in partnership with universities in the region than take on HE numbers herself. She said:

> We see ourselves as interestingly placed here. We are a long way from any university so we have a geographical imperative to offer more locally based opportunities at level four and beyond, and we do definitely see that as part of our mission to widen opportunities to HE in partnership with local universities. We are involved in a consortium that is looking at widening participation. We work very closely with schools on widening participation and with the universities ... I think there are people who would love us to become the university in the town. My real view is that it is a very good thing to widen locally based HE provision but I think our existing route to doing that is incremental and in partnership with the universities. That way we can maintain the quality and the rigour necessary ... Let's take those steps gradually and see where they lead us ...
>
> My concern is to get a lot more people involved and genuinely widen participation so people who wouldn't traditionally have come into HE, or even FE, do so and stick with it and get more fulfilled lives and better jobs (2000).

The Principal felt that the partnerships with the universities were easy to manage and there was no overlap between the institutions, just mutual interest in providing locally based HE. Partnerships with other FE providers in the surrounding towns was also a developing feature and she highlighted a number of difficulties in these partnerships:

> We are working in a lot of partnerships now on a range of initiatives that we would like to use to further our mission, and our involvement is geared

towards that, especially the regeneration partnership, SRB, [Single Regeneration Budget] and so on. This has been a challenge, to work in a sensible collaborative way together. That has been quite difficult because people are very passionate about their patch, their interest group and you know we have to be honest about it, there are tensions between people who have exactly the same objectives but work for a different organisation ... In terms of community education, the colleges meet, but there are so many others who have a need to have a voice in this, so that all needs managing and it is a challenge, with different colleges claiming different organisations as 'their' partners (2000).

She went on to tell me what she thinks works in a partnership:

A few things that I think work: if people on the ground have respect for each other ... that works really well. We have one example of that at the moment on the housing estates that surround the town. People are genuinely coming up with things. Tasks are allocated to each partner and respect for each other is growing. At quite a different level, I think that if there is external funding, different funding, which people can access only if they work in partnership, it works, but I would want to qualify that by saying if you don't get the ground rules right, and get the structures right, and the content right it can go disastrously wrong (2000).

Again, this Principal emphasises structures and clarity of purpose. She was very focused on a co-ordinated approach to partnership, possibly reflective of her approach to management in the college. The college now has clear targets for widening access. The work is monitored and evaluated by the Director of Access and Student Services who, in turn, is accountable to the senior management team. The new structure is now working well and access targets are beginning to be met through the growth of partnership working. The college needed to establish a structure where widening participation could begin to take hold before they were able to meet new participation targets. Although the Principal emphasised that the process of change management had at times been messy, I was struck as I left the college by how clearly defined the process has been. This made me realise that in a situation where transformation is required, managers need to be aware of the goals they wish to achieve but equally importantly they need to have a clear idea of the stages along the way towards their final goal.

The last college studied, Capital College, is different again. Here, the College had a mature widening participation focus and the Principal wanted to encourage innovation to achieve greater success in progression for students by creating a more inclusive college.

Capital College – developing inclusivity

The smallest of the colleges studied and based in the east of the capital, this college attracts 6,000 students, each year of which 78 per cent are from minority ethnic communities. Of the students, 80 per cent live locally and over half of the student population are adults, and over half are women. Focusing entirely on FE provision, the college offers a comprehensive range of general FE with 81 full-time and 229 part-time courses each year. They employ 560 staff and have an annual budget of £14million. They work with a range of partners including regeneration agencies, schools, universities and community organisations. The college is highly regarded and is recognised for its successful work in widening access. The Principal has been in post for nine years and is keen to encourage college staff to reflect regularly on their development. In 1999, she engaged the college in a major revision of its working practices to enable greater flexibility for both students and staff. She wanted the college to re-think its spatial arrange-ments and structural processes to allow for greater creativity. She argued that this would enable the college to be more successful in achieving its mission 'to remove barriers to learning for everyone'.

Unlike Seaside College, Capital College had been involved in access work for many years but the Principal felt that new approaches would benefit the development of their widening participation agenda. I began by asking her what her priorities for widening participation in the college were:

> In terms of widening participation, you could say this college does it all the
> time, because about 95 per cent of our students come from relevant
> postcodes! So what more can we do? Well, that isn't enough, I don't think
> that is the only way you can see widening participation, how many of our
> students get to go to the University of London to study to be doctors? ...
> They want to be doctors and lawyers and we need to enable that ...
> Widening participation is ... also about what access women have to the
> curriculum, such as engineering, and also about their success rate. I want
> to break down those sorts of barriers ... but there are also access issues ...
> At least 70 per cent of local adults currently choose not to study at all.
> That's an access issue for us (1999).

The Principal identified that widening participation in the college needed to be re-organised if it was to continue to be successful. In an internal document, *Removing Barriers for Everyone*, she set out her five priorities to enable their mission to be achieved. These were new ways of working, challenging prejudice, making learning inclusive, making learning accessible and working in partnership.

At the heart of her new ways of working was the development of open-plan office arrangements. She herself worked within the open-plan office of the administration section. Additionally, expanded social space for staff was devel-oped to create informal opportunities for staff to talk and develop ideas. Managed learning environments and group communication via an intranet were also established to enable a more distinct knowledge-management system in the college. She told me why she saw the process as important:

> In the past, considerable effort and energy has been consumed through line
> management structures at the expense of team development. New
> arrangements allow for more delegation to groups of teaching staff led by
> heads of programme. New arrangements for management meetings
> encourage greater involvement and networking (1999).

Her college functions through good clear communication systems, which have been constructed by developing new spatial relationships between workers and students and through redesigning how meetings and teaching occurs. She told me:

> The structure is largely flat. We have an almost wholly female senior management team, which is actually quite unusual. We only have two men in the team. All meetings throughout the college are published and key themes for each meeting are posted so that if someone has something to say on that issue they can prepare for it, and everyone knows what topics are being discussed. I don't believe in having 'Chairs' for meetings. They waste time, so each item has someone's name attached to it and it is their responsibility to keep to time for that item. It works, too.
>
> Clarity, you see, clarity of goals, of job descriptions, of what is expected ... It is the only fair way to be (1999).

Pritchard (2000, p 45) points out that the organisation of space can significantly affect the way an organisation is managed. He says: 'The spatiality of the desk, the physicality of the suit and the team briefing can be read ... the different spatiality of pre and post meeting discussions, even the training events are sites [for] potential new orderings ...'

In other words, the everyday experience of our work environment communicates the values of the organisation. It produces particular ways of working and encourages certain taken-for-granted practices. Lecturers are well aware of the significance of the layout of classrooms. The Principal was using these same ideas across the whole college. She went on to tell me about the shifting to an open-plan college:

> The administrative area works really well. The teaching ones need more work. We have no offices; it is about accessibility, about being structured into clear teams, providing work areas for those teams to think together, some closed and some open. We see them as a way to enable people to work on problems together. They also provide resource bases, which are often the hub of the area. Each base has its own refreshment area. In fact, I must say the free refreshments was sort of what sold the idea to the teaching staff, but I do think it is a rather creative way of people informally looking at problems. It is structured so that people who do relate to each other are able to meet informally to help them work on problems. Also, it is about accessibility for students. That is part of widening participation for us, accessibility (1999).

Writing about HE, Taylor (1995, p 197) points out that student diversity should be matched by staff diversity, creating 'an atmosphere and [providing] role models that may encourage them [the students] to become more engaged'. In examining her four areas to develop in the college, inclusion in learning was a priority for the Principal. She felt that more could be done to encourage more lecturing staff from local communities to work in the college. She introduced a Bangladeshi teacher-training scheme to train an additional two graduates a year to change the profile of the teachers significantly by 2004. She saw accessible learning as not only being about where and when courses were offered, but also about improving the quality of teaching itself:

> We have recently introduced compulsory classroom observation because I want quality in this college. Teaching needs to be of a high standard, meeting the needs of students, but we need staff to know the parameters not just inspect them. Show them what we expect and then measure our success. We do this through teaching staff meeting with their manager twice a year to set goals, to review developments and to plan for the future. We have a learning-and-teaching area for staff to raise issues that have come up. This provides a more informal space to enable people to be creative to find solutions, not really based on conventional staff development (1999).

The Principal wanted to transform the environment to enable learners rather than the learners having to adapt to the environment. I asked her if she thought I had understood it right:

> MS: *You seem to tackle the need for change in the college head on. Many of the colleges I have visited seem to have kept many of the more old fashioned management practices but you seem to have tried to draw on a range of newer management strategies, like the open plan, like supporting creative informal solutions, and so on ...*

> Principal: It hasn't always been easy to push forward change. I've had real difficulty with reshaping the work. Many of the staff have had to completely reconceptualise how they deliver learning to students, but after all, that is what we wanted to achieve, but it hasn't been easy (1999).

Pritchard (2000, p 174) points out that women managers are more likely to take change forward and are often more appreciative of different approaches: 'Women's relative outsider positioning – their lack of loyalty to the "established ways of doing things" – means that they become highly valued managers for change in a new environment.'

Rather than resting on the laurels of her success in widening participation, the Principal was working on new challenges. She was always looking out for new approaches to improve her college's performance. She had taken the notion of new ways of working into her widening participation activities. She told me that if 70 per cent of local people would not come to the college or their community centres, then the college must go to where the people did go – supermarkets. She revealed:

> In order to attract these people into learning, we have established Idea Stores adjacent to major supermarkets across the borough. Idea Stores look and feel like retail outlets but actually offer a library, learning opportunities and IT facilitates. The atmosphere is fabulous and doesn't feel at all like the world of 'school', to make it ordinary ... you pick up your shopping and you pick up a course or whatever (1999).

The examples from the three colleges are diverse and are rooted in the needs of each institution, its stage of development in widening participation terms and its locality. In Northern City College, great emphasis is placed on working in communities and sustaining partnerships with the local communities. The systems in that college emphasise relationship building and communication. Widening participation in this context was about access and involving local people in the college. Diversity in the community was reproduced in the staff at the college and, as head of a mature institution, the Principal had clear support mechanisms in place for staff working in communities.

Seaside College, on the other hand, was at a much earlier stage of development. The college needed to develop the structures to enable widening participation. Hence, a major restructuring was required. The Principal concentrated on developing strategy and getting endorsement for the strategy before tackling structural change. Capital College's focus was more on progression for and retention of the students, hence the Principal wanted to create a system where colleagues in the institution could ensure that their teaching was of a high standard and that new ideas could develop and flourish. She was clear that bringing staff together in their physical workspace was a vital resource that could be tapped to produce innovation in practice. She redesigned work-spaces within and, through her supermarket initiative, beyond the college to enable innovation in widening participation practice to grow.

There is no one right way to manage widening participation in FE but the colleges discussed here do provide examples of practice that could be adapted to different situations. Clarity of purpose and understanding what elements of widening participation need particular attention are key to designing the appropriate structures and systems for any manager in an institution. Despite their different needs, however, all the professionals interviewed highlighted the value of education as a life-enhancing process and argued that widening participation was the main reason why they were involved in education. The Principal of Northern City College captured this sentiment exactly when he said:

> I do believe that education is a liberator and it gives people more choice about how they deal with things I'm going to give you an example. I went to do a 'keynote' at an Access Graduation Day a couple of weeks back ... a lot of students who were there were students who had been at the youth club I ran many years ago ... hard cases, difficult kids, drop-outs at school, and I went in there and now they have kids of their own and they were just finishing their Access course.
>
> I said 'what you doing now?' and they said 'I've got choices. I could go to this university or to that university' and I can see these people six, seven years ago, and they say now, 'you know what – what's so wonderful, when the kids come home from school with their homework, I can do their homework. I can question the headmistress about things' and you know, it made the hairs on the back of my head stand up seeing those 'kids' that wouldn't go to school when they were young, and now there they were, saying 'I can go in to school and I can intervene' ... because even if they don't get a degree or a job the cycle's broken (1999).

I began the chapter talking about the Cinderella story. Perhaps the other element of FE being a Cinderella service is its capacity to act as a Fairy Godmother to students. The case studies in this chapter have provided some of the magic that can be used to provide new learners with the skills and knowledge to leave the kitchen and get to the ball. This transformative power is potentially enormous.

The next chapter examines practice in HEIs.

6 Making the unseen university visible – widening participation case studies from higher education

Universities have always been places where local people may go to work but not necessarily places where they go to study. Widening participation in HE requires universities to be seen in their communities. It also requires academics to see their communities as potential student markets. Visibility is about internal and external 'magic'. It is about transforming cultures within institutions whose mission has been to provide for a small elite of people who have succeeded through a conventional learning pathway. Widening participation in HE is also about communities who have not seen higher-level learning as important to their lives beginning to value a university education. The case studies in this chapter, like the previous chapter on FE, focus on different styles and approaches to widening participation. Again, I am not suggesting that any of the following examples present superior practice to others. Different approaches are vital because universities and colleges operate in very different circumstances. Rather, these case studies provide different methods of tackling widening participation in their institutions, which could be adapted to different circumstances.

The British HE environment has shifted significantly since the early 1990s. Nearly all the old polytechnics are now universities. Yet, the removal of the binary divide has not really altered the map of HE. Universities have split themselves, despite the appearance of a united front through Universities UK, into three different groups: the Russell group, a group of universities which are regarded as elite universities; the 1994 group, which largely contains the new, old universities and the Modern Universities group, a group for many of the new, new universities. There remain considerable differences and inequalities between institutions that now all share the title of 'university'.

This chapter provides examples of approaches to widening participation from all three groupings of universities, emphasising my belief that, despite the fact that universities will respond to widening participation in different ways, widening participation is a sector-wide issue. In this chapter, I highlight the importance of visibility as the key to any approach to widening participation in HE. The title of this chapter is taken from the fictional world of the

Disc created by Terry Pratchett. In *Discworld*, the wizards have a university but the people of the capital city, Ank-morpork, cannot see it. It is invisible. It is a place filled with magic, so much magic that the books have to be chained down. Female witches have (of course) only recently been allowed into the university, but even they have not made it visible to the people in the city. The trick, for our real-life universities is to make themselves visible to people who would not conceive of higher education as a possibility. Visibility in this context is not just about seeing, it is also about believing, believing that you can be part of the academy, and that the academy will engage with you.

The following case studies show how different universities have used part-nerships to develop engagement with their communities. They provide examples of change-management approaches to facilitate greater flexibility in access and participation. Three main approaches can be detected from the universities studied. The first can be described as a whole-university approach, led from the top by the senior management. Here, the senior staff drive the direction of widening participation allocating responsibility across the institu-tion. Another approach is to develop central services that mediate between the communities and academic units, creating a user-friendly staff group who can relate to cultures in and outside the institution. The third method uses the expertise of specific staff, as in the second model, but places the responsibility for developing widening participation in the hands of a particular academic unit. Each of these methods produces different results, and each has its merits. Universities do have differing missions and will respond in line with their vision of themselves, but if widening participation is to mean anything in higher education, universities need to engage with the diversity of the commu-nities that surround them in Britain today. Each of the case studies presented in this chapter suggests alternative approaches to engaging with our communities. The first study is an example of a whole-institution response to widening participation.

Leading from the centre – strategy and the role of partnership in change

Based in the heart of the capital, this new university has approximately 8,000 full-time students and 6,000 part-time students in any one year. Capital City university has a strong mix of minority ethnic students and a more or less equal gender balance. The business school has the largest curriculum area for the university. A major re-organisation led to a dual mission to serve the business community of London and a desire to work in partnership with communities local to the university. They attract a significant sum from the funding council's postcode analysis. Their Rector was determined to examine how they could use the funding to broaden and deepen their involvement in future widening partici-pation activities. He pointed out to me that the local area which the university served was both 'one of the most rich areas of the world and one of the poorest of the European Union' (1999). The university, he said, straddled 'a huge divide in British society' (1999).

The university has targeted specific low participation areas where they hoped to recruit more students. The university drew on the expertise of its own students to act as ambassadors in these areas. Students who come from these neighbourhoods go back into their previous schools to work with the kids in the area, providing role models for the young people. The Rector felt that this sort of aspiration-raising work was a good example of how going to university could be seen as the next automatic step for children who had previously not considered higher education. Unlike the examples detailed in new research (Utley, 2001), which points out that much of the current aspiration-raising work is simply identifying students who would be likely to go on to university in any case, this project created links between young people and students from the same low-participation neighbourhood with similar life experiences.

Capital City University sees widening participation as central to its mission and has taken its commitment to partnership in the local region seriously, with the Vice-Rector being the chair of the local regeneration partnership. The partnership has been operating for some time, using the Single Regeneration Budget for a range of projects to support the area. The Vice Rector told me:

> With SRB-4, we had a very large employability programme and the university and the college here are involved. It developed two strands; the one was to break the stereotypes of our students to enable graduates to have a better deal of getting jobs and the other is called 'work-based development' where we buy up work space and make it affordable for new start-ups (1999).

The partnership is not simply about education and students, as he went on to emphasise:

> The next phase of this will be major programmes on housing redevelopment, refurbishing even demolishing and then rebuilding low-level housing. So, it is very ambitious. We have £45million specifically from SRB but this is the tip of the iceberg. We want ten times more than that, but even so, the whole regeneration project is quite powerful (1999).

For the senior managers of this university, developing a local profile and being committed to development in the local area is a central part of their widening participation strategy. The Rector explained:

> The university is locked into this as we are chairing the partnership and also through the employability work with businesses and a whole host of other projects. I think that is what I mean; you can't simply say we will recruit people from the ethnic minority communities and not do anything else. You can not do that. You have to have a whole-institution strategy to participate in the community in a whole variety of ways, and therefore lock yourself into the community (1999).

Working with local people at a senior level was a major part of the university's strategy. I asked the Rector to outline how they had moved from being what was considered a more conventional university to being a university where local people felt more comfortable. He explained the transition in this way:

Until the late 1980s, the polytechnic was a very traditional institution but unusual in the major respect that it was the first 'university' in the country to take on the modular system, so the university had a flexible programme, but, in terms of the range of subjects the university provided it was quite traditional ... So I suppose the first major change was just before I came to the university in the late eighties when they decided that it was no longer tenable to offer as wide a range of traditional programmes as previously. The university decided to re-think its provision. Those decisions were taken in the context of what the role of a city university should be.

... When we had a financial crisis, we had to focus our minds and, at that point, we focused on the mission to serving London, both in terms of teaching and in research ...

The reason why we have made significant progress across the institution is that it coincided with the ... arrival of Objective II status ... particularly within the area that we were in ... We held a brainstorming session with the local Training and Enterprise Council and the Department for Trade and Industry and some initiatives came out of that, so when we wanted to take advantage of the new funds, we could at least say that we are doing something ... We developed from there.

We saw ourselves as not just a university in the conventional sense but felt we could be involved in serious regeneration. We got into a range of projects with funding from different pots ... We realised we could make things happen in different ways and enabled us individually through networks and partnerships to change the way we function in relation to our communities (1999).

Partnership working became extremely important to enabling the changes that were required in the university:

The reality is that we are probably named as a partner in about around 30 partnerships, which is not untypical but is unusual for a university. We always aim to be part of the changing agenda. We also have to influence the change and, increasingly, people are turning to us and saying that they want this or that. This means that when opportunities do arise, we do not have to scrabble around asking people what they want. We have got them. And that is efficiency in my book as we know who we can trust, we know who has a good track record and with whom we do not want to deal. And we have to keep our eye on the ball and say it is all in aid of strengthening the institution's presence in the community. I think that is the best way we can achieve it (Vice Rector, 1999).

For the senior managers in this university, external opportunities and internal pressures were the drivers for change. Developing and using external contacts was central to winning the case within the university. This suggests that change management from the top, as this university developed, still required champions beyond the initiators. In this environment, the senior managers used external contacts and other forms of government/public sector developments to drive the change within the institution. The senior managers went on to discuss how change within the university was a complex, and sometimes slow, process, as the Vice-Rector told me:

> We need to face up to the fact that the skill sets that most of our staff have is not fit for purpose. We can trade off a lot of things against it but we will not widen participation properly. Widening participation must be linked with improving prospects and this is where the role of the academic comes in ... You have to give people the tools to deal with it and we do not have them ... One point we have recognised is the reality of that and as far as possible we must engage our own staff ... They are finding the work different. We have to help them with personal development. But we also recognise that we can't do that for all internal courses so we have brought people in, appointed people from other places who have the skills. We have created a Learning and Development Unit, which has proved very successful and is creating a new cultural environment (1999).

Once the changed external environment had been recognised by staff, the senior managers began to lead a cultural change within the institution. For them, internal change required a process of offering staff development, bringing in new expertise and enabling a shared culture between different groups to develop. The Vice Rector went on to argue:

> The Learning and Development Unit has been very successful. It was originally seen as something very separate from the work of academics, but students would go to them for help. Now, as the culture has shifted, the academics have asked for help to incorporate modules into their own programmes and that provides the on-course support that students need (1999).

For managers in higher education, this university-wide approach highlights the importance of senior level commitment to the development of widening partici-pation, but even more interesting here is the interplay between internal and external collaborations which provided the climate for change that the senior managers required. It is a useful strategy in any university environment to work with outsiders to build alliances that create a climate of change within the university. Partnerships in this environment helped the university to be visible in their locale and helped university staff to see how their locale could benefit them. Whole-university approaches are usually led by Vice Chancellors or Rectors, as in Capital City University, but in different circumstances, other units in a university may be more appropriate to act as champions of change.

Marginality and central planning – continuing education and widening participation

Continuing education (CE) departments in old universities have a long tradition of working in partnership with their local communities and in attempting to widen access to higher education. Their role in many such universities has been to provide a link with the local community, usually working with adults returning to study on a part-time basis but also working outside the conventional university framework. As discussed in Chapter 3, being in a marginal position to the rest of the university is to enjoy an ambivalent position. Marginality is a space that offers a high degree of flexibility and creative opportunities, but it can also reduce the ability to influence the wider organisation. However, as Duke has identified, continuing education has been a significant change agent in HE over the past 50 or so years. He says (1994, p 223): 'CE is a kind of experimental site to test innovations which may then be adopted more widely with the university.'

The next two examples have used CE departments very differently to develop their universities' mission to widen participation. The first example used the Director of Continuing Education as the champion to lead a whole university change process to widen the participation of their local communities in the university.

Reshaping the whole university from the margins

When a new Vice Chancellor came to this small university in a northern city, he re-shaped the mission of the University towards the local community. Northern University was the only university in the city and the Vice Chancellor felt that it must fulfil its social imperative to support its local community. Recognising that this re-organisation would require a specific champion for widening participation the Vice Chancellor took the opportunity in 1999 to create a new university-wide post for lifelong learning and widening participation, drawing together the role of Director of the continuing education department and university widening participation leadership. The Centre for Continuing Education has been working in the locality since the university was established. It had developed extensive partnership arrangements with the youth service and local communities in the area, providing new educational opportunities on demand. The new director of the centre had considerable experience of change management processes, having been part of a major re-organisation in a new university. He saw a range of challenges in his role, particularly recognising that change within an old university required a different approach to his previous work:

> There is amazing difference between the new and the old universities
> because new universities come across as really corporate bodies with clear
> lines of responsibilities, but people don't necessarily do what they have
> been told to do. Instead, they develop strategies to avoid doing what they
> have been told to do while in the old universities, because there is
> consensus and collegiality it is much more difficult to argue and put your
> barriers up as you are then outside the consensus. The consensus in the
> new universities might be 'we must not let the management win, we must
> not give in' whereas in the old universities, by making the decisions
> through consensus, it creates a different set of relationships. I have no idea
> how a PVC or a Dean operates when they return to their substantive post.
> On the other hand, in this system, you also limit the amount of new blood

coming in, and when new blood does come in, they have to spend time getting to know the university, to understand it (2000).

The process of change here was one that centred on persuasion and argument. Using the expertise of staff in the Centre for Continuing Education who had learned to work in partnership with local communities and who understood the needs of local people was vital to this approach. I asked the Director how he understood widening participation:

> It's a term I'd like to abolish. It is a term that is much over-used often simply to measure the numbers of students who come in. We need to shift away from that because it is dead easy to say we have so many registered and I would rather have something that talked about equity and how you support students through the system, rather than what some people call widening participation.
>
> I would ensure that progression was both horizontal and vertical and I think we need far greater clarity on targeting because I don't think we have that right. I don't think it is about gender or ethnicity – it is particularly about social class and if you look at social class four and five, where is the participation? That goes across the board. I think disability is probably outside of that and should be included. I think something on equity and social inclusion is a more useful concept (2000).

He saw the issues for this university were to be responsive to local need and to develop courses that local people would want. Drawing on the expertise already within his department and his own experience of inner city work, he began to explore ways of influencing change in the university:

> It was a major opportunity ... working in the inner city, which is crucial to me, to work very much with disadvantaged groups and to try and change practice cause the amount of change possible here is dramatic, because in an area of such disadvantage to only have an old university is unusual. The University is okay in terms of student recruitment in relation to the sector but if you do that measurement in relation to the local area, it's not so good. So I wanted to deal with that because it is not about a particular bolt-on part of the university; it is about putting a new university model about lifelong learning into an old university, and I am still really excited about that ... I've never really explained it like that before, new university culture to an old university because that is too simple, but that is sort of what I am doing (2000).

The department is organised with its own student numbers and is engaged in a number of projects with the youth service in the city as well as working with local community groups to train activists as community development workers. The Director was keen to use the centre as a catalyst for change across the university, not to see the centre as the main focus for widening participation work:

> If you do that, it may make the other schools say 'ah ha, lifelong learning is being taken care of by that bit and we don't have to do it'. Part of the

change that's taking place within the university can be seen in how they re-organised for my appointment. They wanted the role to manage the centre on a Monday and the other four days of the week to work across the institution developing lifelong learning. I know this model, as it is something I am more used to and I am quite happy to focus on the institution wide activity, but also have the centre to fall back on as a delivery unit. It's an interesting discussion and debate and you can see what is happening. People want to shift part-time undergraduates across to Continuing Education because they are harder to manage, but we don't want that. It is important that it is a university-wide initiative (2000).

The strategy was to use the centre to respond quickly to demands in the community while working more slowly to transform other areas of the university. The centre was pivotal to change in the university. It led by example. Academic staff from the centre worked with other colleagues to develop new learning strategies and different modes of study to attract new learners. The Director went on to emphasise that to be successful the university needed to monitor its performance in recruitment and retention in the same way as other areas of teaching. This gave the work status and prevented it being seen as a kind of add-on to the mainstream of university work:

We need to measure through quality assurance and other systems, in the mainstream ... its something we have learned from the disability movement. We can't have conversations any more about how we can't let a hearing-impaired person in, well I hope we can't. The focus has shifted. It is now about how we can support them. And there's a whole series of issues around changing language and changing culture there with regard to support (2000).

The university has since developed 'compacts' with local schools and runs a successful junior university for local children each year. A compact for local residents in the city, offering an entitlement to HE, has also been worked out with the city council and part-time learning opportunities are now available across the institution. Unlike this university, where the approach was to encourage all parts of the university to develop widening participation activities, the next case study is based on a model where the CE department provides the major link with the locality and delivers the majority of the university's widening participation strategy.

Continuing education as widening participation

Midlands University is based in the heart of England and has been working with the local community developing part-time degrees and study opportunities for many years. An early advocate of Access courses, its CE department established a partnership arrangement with local FE colleges to develop 2 + 2 degree programmes in the early 1980s. In 2000, they were successful in gaining funding to develop a prototype foundation degree in community development in partnership with local colleges and voluntary sector community workers. The university as a whole has a student profile that is reminiscent of other research-intensive universities with their undergraduate intake coming substantially from social classes one and two. Their key aim in widening participation centred on the development of part-time study routes and the Centre for CE took a lead role in this work. The Head of Department put it this way:

> So what does widening participation mean in our context? Here, it has to be part time, there is little chance that my university will be really interested in local people in the full-time market (1999).

Although the university does participate in aspiration-raising summer schools and some other types of activities for school-aged children to widen participation, their core focus is around the development of part-time study modes as a mechanism for widening participation. The Head of Department has developed alliances and partnerships both within and beyond his institution. He was one of the key people involved in local and regional partnerships. He told me:

> We were involved in two SRB areas. The more interesting one we were involved with was the Urban Partnership in a multi-ethnic area. My colleague chaired that partnership. We had to be careful not to flood them with bids from the university. It makes sense to get cash going into the community. The university is maturing and growing up. One of the nice things about that is that the university does not have to be so insecure and not so brash. It can, and should, as a relatively good enterprise with a strong public service ethos mission, support community growth ... You have an obligation to the local area, in our case a strong one (1999).

Their work in partnership has not sought to favour the university but to take a long-term view. Some might argue that that is easy for a rich old university but in reality, it is not that dissimilar to the approach taken by Capital City University. Partnership working must be long term and is not just about education, but rather about whole-area regeneration. The recognition that universities and colleges need to take on activities in partnership that may initially seem unrelated to their core activities throws up the idea of permeability again. Education can no longer be seen as separate from other social services and needs to be planned in relation to the needs of the whole society.

Midlands University had entrusted the CE department with the main role for widening participation and they were encouraged to take the agenda forward as they saw fit. The Head of Department identified three areas for widening participation development over the course of the interview:

> I think we can push in three major directions. One is the FE area which is strongly developed; we have good networks, which grew out of the Open College Network and as a result of that and building the 2 +2 degree on top of that we have good relations with all the colleges. The colleges value that relationship and we value it ... but we need to make it more substantial. One particularly interesting development is the creative research partnership with associated colleges that we have developed. It is good in terms of bringing in funding but also engaging the colleges in

determining the research agenda and in one project putting the money back into the colleges for their staff to do research (1999).

This form of partnership brings together the skills in a research-intensive university with the skills of FE colleges who work more closely with the communities in the area. It offers the colleges a change to develop their practice through reflection and it provides a two-way understanding of issues around progression. Research is an area that many universities can offer to their partners in developing widening participation but it seems that few are able to see the relevance of working locally. Quinn (2001) points out universities' RAE focus on publishing in journals has mitigated against academics working for communities. She says (2001, p 14):

> The main community issues to emerge from a recent survey were not social inclusion, but drugs, housing, planning and crime. These are topics in which many HEIs are undertaking research, yet how far is this known in local communities, or relayed to them?

Developed over ten years ago, this further–higher education partnership attracts funding for new research projects and is growing all the time. Staff from FE and the university meet together to discuss findings and work is often jointly published. While this sort of research partnership is not unique it is still relatively unusual in Britain. Other radical examples can be found in other countries such as Australia. One such project works with students as partners to research widening access issues:

> Teachers, community members and university researchers can contribute different benefits to the process of collaboration. Community representatives can be an excellent source of cultural knowledge and provide the ability to solve conflicts in values and working style; teachers can provide excellent sources of knowledge about the students and the school culture. Finally, university researchers may contribute to the processes and evaluation of action research activities (Atweh and Bland, 1999, p 33).

Widening participation for universities and colleges should not just increase student numbers, even if they do come from the right areas. It should also provide opportunities to investigate successful engagements with new learners and their communities. Collaborative research can and should be part of the ongoing development of widening participation. It should propose new ways of working, new partnerships, new arrangements to support the growth of learning in a society. This type of project should increase if widening participation is to take hold seriously in universities. It will produce practice that is more informed and enable greater innovation. While there are national surveys and national research projects, local and regional collaborative research initiatives should be supported by individual universities as a way of contributing to widening participation in education.

There were two other areas that the Head of CE at Midlands University outlined that his CE department was developing to support widening participation:

The second area is community based; there was not as much happening as a couple of years ago. I think we can start afresh and look at foundation degrees as the way forward here. We are starting out right next to this campus; the other side of that fence on the estate. There is a history, this campus was where they built hostels for women and all the factories were down this side of the city so in order to build spaces for bombed-out populations they built the estates. This side of the city there are 4,000 jobs in the industry around the campus and virtually none of the jobs are taken by local people. So we are looking to work with the local regeneration partnership and local colleges to do some outreach work. We are going ahead with foundation degrees, one in community work. So there is a lot of interest with that in the university and I can see it starting with community-based outreach which will involve the Schools and Colleges Liaison Service in the University. That is how we work here. We establish the parameters and then we bring in other parts of the university when it is appropriate (2000).

Working outside the university as a mediator in this way facilitates access for people who often find the structures within universities difficult to comprehend. It provides a friendly face who can help people in the community navigate their way through the system. Staff working in CE have specific expertise to work in the community and are much better placed to reach out than conventional academics.

The third area of widening participation work for this department was part-time study – working with employers to increase the skills and expertise of their workers. Again the Head of Department emphasised that having established the links and developed the work, many of the partnerships would become the responsibility of the central university:

The third part of our widening participation strategy is take on employers in the private sector, not that the department is responsible for all of the continuing vocational education in the university as we have down-sized that responsibility ... As a result of raising this with the Academic Registrar, we said it would not be a central part of our work and we would not be able to give it the attention it deserved but we have brokered many of the partnerships and we have highlighted the widening participation angle; now it's over to them ... Our focus is on training and human resource activities. We have the expertise and it is a way of promoting lifelong learning in the workplace. In that area, we will increase (2000).

In Midlands University, the Department for CE directs widening participation. Their position between the rest of the university and the locale enables them to advise the University on widening participation. The key element of their widening participation strategy is to focus on part-time study, which the Head of Department felt would be the most effective way for the university to contribute to widening participation. The Department is also expected to provide a university presence in the area. The freedom that the department has to deliver widening participation is potentially risky for the university, but it also offers the opportunity for greater flexibility and new innovation. Some have criticised old universities for not being committed to widening participation. In some cases, this is true, but using a vibrant CE department as the core of the university's widening participation strategy has its strengths. It will not produce a whole-university transformation, but it will offer innovation in part-time learning, which some argue needs to be a significant element of widening participation strategies if government targets are to be reached.

The final examples of widening participation in universities comes from two new universities. These case studies show how centrally developed services can create the necessary links to the community and also how universities use these services as a major planning tool for development.

Centrally located services – 'In-reach'

Located in the heart of a large northern city, Yorkshire University has a large undergraduate population. Their marketing strategy relies heavily on a widening participation mission to recruit its target numbers. The University developed an Access and Guidance Service to facilitate this mission. My interviewee was the Co-ordinator of the service. She saw her role as both a supporter of students and as a change agent in the university. Needing to work in partnership with the local community to increase the number of students applying to the University, the Access and Guidance Service became crucially important:

> When I first came here, guidance had grown out of the access work. For it to be really effective, we had to work alongside people to help them explore and create opportunities as well as just making choices; making choices assumes you have reached a certain stage. So we are working at the point where we are responding to people who are just asking about HE and also in communities where people have no connection with HE at all. And we might be bringing them and their kids into the university and saying this is what the unit is for and its function, or we could stay within the community and think of looking at ways we can look in the context of community organisations.
>
> Given change in recruitment patterns and given the low average for staying-on rates in this area, it seems that strategic view is about survival for the university (1999).

Like the first example in this chapter, my interviewee in this university emphasised the point that partnership with external groups can create change within organisations:

> I also sought to get involved in external networks, whose existence I thought could provide a lever to the university from outside. And one of the key areas was working with kids and parents in schools and getting out and talking to parent groups, so that money enabled us to get out and talk to primary schools. Now we are out of that, we have appointed community education development officers who work with those partners

> and bring groups to the university. Certainly for the university, yes, partnership is important. There are some things that we can do on our own and internal partnership is just as important (1999).

Unlike Capital City University, however, the driver for change here was from the second tier of management as new ideas and expertise were coming from contacts developed by the staff in the Access and Guidance Service. Having placed the service at the centre of the university's work, these staff members found their voices were being listened to. They used the demands of the local community as a lever for change within the university.

Much of the literature on change management emphasises the role of senior managers in creating new developments. It is not always the case that senior managers need to lead change. In an organisation that encourages development, any staff member can initiate change and innovation. As I argued in Chapter 3, management is a team-driven process where collaboration between staff will often produce long-lasting and innovative practice. Change will take hold in an organisation where staff can see the need for a different approach to achieve its aims. Having recognised its need to tap the local market for students, this university relied on the managers in its Access and Guidance Service to identify and lead the change necessary to make this happen. Drawing on the right expertise wherever this lies is vital to the success of any widening participation strategy. Knowing where this expertise lies and trusting their judgement is the challenge for many senior managers. In the final case study, this point was equally important. My interviewee stressed the need for trust to be a two-way process between senior staff and their change agents:

> We are lucky, we have a fair bit of autonomy in relation to what we do and where we are placed. I do not take that for granted at all and we use that autonomy to the best effect, both in terms of work within the centre and in terms of its relationship to other bits of the university, and external work. We see that as a positive thing, that the university provides for us that autonomy. I value it and I know that other people here value it (1999).

It is unusual for a new university to have a centre for continuing education but our final example of widening participation practice, Central University, has a small but vibrant Continuing Education Centre, which works across the university's widening participation initiatives. Established in 1991, the centre has been active in research into widening participation and has been involved in local partnerships and projects to support increased participation in higher education for many years. The Director represents the university on a variety of local, regional and national bodies. Clearly, as several of the examples in this chapter have shown, middle management has a significant role to play in many universities' approaches to widening participation. However, the Director told me that he felt that widening participation was well established at his university, having developed the work over a period of ten years. He said:

> I have been here ten years and it has always been a major part of the work we do and I am proud of the university because I think it has been a major

contributor to opening up opportunities to local people. It has a firm commitment and that is measurable. That, for me, is a comfortable way of working in terms of widening participation. This university has a good track record. Now that the agenda has changed, our work has come together more. The funding and political agenda help. In the past, sometimes you felt you were ploughing a very lonely furrow as what the university did was out of sync, but that did not stop us doing it and continuing with it. We have not had to do the hearts-and-minds change to widening participation that I see other institutions doing. We have not had to do that as the nature of this university is to provide opportunities to a broad range of local people, so in terms of the internal and external interface, hopefully it will get easier for us (1999).

The position of the centre and its Director has changed as external pressures on developing widening participation have changed. The centre is responsible for the accreditation of prior (experiential) learning (AP[E]L) in the university and has a national reputation in this area. I asked the Director how the centre fitted into the rest of the university:

The centre has a number of responsibilities agreed by the university. We have many areas where we lead or are major contributors. This is important to us because it gives us a focus for work and is important in terms of how we relate to the university at large.

We have an influencing, lobbying and departmental role in a number of areas like widening participation, but we have been involved in that before it was called widening participation, so there is nothing new there. However, there is now a different emphasis and external interest in widening participation especially with the lead from the funding council, which has implications on how the university conducts itself with widening participation. That is one example of how we are in the forefront guiding, supporting and initiating things across the university, working with the external pulls and pushes towards widening participation and access in general (1999).

The new role for the centre has given them the responsibility of changing behaviour within the university to enable departments to be more successful in both attracting and retaining diverse students. The Director went on to say:

Another area where we will revise and work with colleagues, schools and courses is on how they can access different kinds of students as well as on what basis they come to us. One of our purposes is to encourage innovation and different behaviour of the university as I think these are really important, as it is not what people say but what they do that really counts. We focused on changing behaviour in various ways in line with our agreed area of responsibilities within the centre. So that is the major function that we play (1999).

The Director also emphasised the centre's role in working with groups outside the university. He said that he saw 'the only way you can do widening participation is by working in partnership' and that this was an important area in the work of the centre:

> One of the roles is as a mediator between communities, potential students and the university ... so what I am saying in relation to widening participation is there are ways of working that enable us to learn from students and it is interesting to hear what they have to say (1999).

Developing relationships and enabling encounters to affect practice helped innovation to develop in the university. I asked him to provide me with a concrete example:

> The partnerships that we develop are informed by the context that we work within. For example, a couple of years ago, we were doing some work around widening provision and someone that I knew from a local tenants' association was trying to set up a range of activities for people of African origin and he struggled to get these going. The group could not get resources from anywhere. I met my contact and we chatted and said that there must be something we can do. From that came a series of things like having IT access on a Saturday morning for the group, which is when they wanted to get together, and also a number of courses. I knew what we had and there was someone who was looking for connection and I think that is what happens with a lot of partnerships we do. Sometimes there are more formal ways but a lot of the time informality works better (1999).

He went on to explain how these partnerships with local people enabled them to gain access to the university:

> Working from that interface between external things and internal issues is about managing, linking and collecting those two things in all kinds of ways. I need to understand how the institution works in a lot of detail and recognise how we can push here and not there. It is quite political in that sense of having a sharp appreciation of how you get things done and using that knowledge for external people is sometimes challenging. I try to do big schemes on a big scale because I am impatient to do things that make a real change rather then piloting the small things.
>
> To use an example of the associate student scheme: it started nine years ago, a couple of years after I came here, so I was very much involved in the beginning of the scheme and it is a simple idea. Where local students enrolled or connected with a college or an adult education outfit we had an agreement with, they could gain access to all the resources in the university in the same way as an undergraduate who came here. So they use the library, counselling, guidance and all that and have access to it when they want to and when they decide they need to. One of the important things is that it is not a course-based offer; it was to say 'here are the resources we have and how can we open them up to local learners?' It gave people who did not know of anyone in their family who had been to the university a chance to get in the door (1999).

The scheme also makes sense in marketing terms. In any one year, the university gets 30 per cent of these associated students registering to do full- or part-time courses. From their follow-up work, the university knows that an even larger number go into some other form of study after the scheme. The Director was convinced that, from watching the scheme develop and the feedback they got from students, the scheme has been important for students, making HE more visible in communities and more possible for individuals.

Each case study discussed in this chapter has approached the idea of university visibility differently and each institution has engaged with the widening participation agenda in the context of their own mission. Some examples are more deeply developed and embedded in the institution and some are newer initiatives. These examples highlight the diversity inherent in the concept of widening participation, not just in HE itself, indicating that 'good practice' is not only about increasing the numbers of students in current HE provision but also about engaging with excluded groups using innovative approaches. If widening participation is to succeed in HE, valuing the diversity of approach to increase participation is vital.

While approaches described here focus on systems and structures in the institutions to create change, strikingly, in each case, the role of individuals, in terms of their commitment and in terms of their abilities to relate to colleagues and external partners, seems to have been highly significant.

The next chapter examines the importance of individual life histories to the development of widening participation in education.

7 Individuals, life experience and leadership

So far I have concentrated on 'practice' within F and HE, often through the reflections of individuals but, all the same, on actual practices. While conducting the research for the book, I became aware that an individual's prior experiences seemed to contribute to their approach to widening participation activities. Of course, this is obvious; individuals make up organisations and their personalities are going to shape some decision making but, in a partnership environment, individuals' personalities will be particularly influential on how relationships are built and maintained.

In this chapter, I focus on the role of leadership in developing widening participation, arguing that passion and individual life experience can create a climate for development. Insufficient attention has been paid to the biographies of individuals in the work environment, as Bagguley (1992) suggests. Very few studies actually examine people's life experiences despite the rhetoric in much of the management literature that emphasises leadership as an essential component of organisational development. This chapter looks at how the life histories and experiences of the individuals I interviewed have affected their work practice. It draws out the similarities between them and suggests that these connections affect the development of their widening participation strategies. Here I also examine the importance of the role of network managers as discussed by Pritchard (2000). He suggests that, as the cultural and social environment of educational institutions has changed, managers require a higher level of social skills. In particular, he highlights the value of networking between individuals and groups. He says such managers who are more focused on broader contacts and links between themselves and others, often outside their own institutions, are more able to help their institutions grow and change. Strong social networks have been, I argue, the most significant factor in initiating and sustaining change and developing widening participation within the organisations studied in this book.

The debate between agency and structure has a long history in the social sciences and has recently been reinvigorated. I do not intend to rehearse debates here except to acknowledge that the interplay between individuals and social structures is inherent to social change. I have already argued in Chapter 3 that material conditions shape the environment that individuals inherit, and here I suggest that beyond that base, individuals have a significant role to play in influencing development. The importance of network managers in organisations has its theoretical base in conceptions of social capital (Bourdieu, 1984) and life history research (Searle-Chatterjee, 1999). Unlike earlier theoretical perspectives, the concept of network managers does not propose a class-limited notion of social capital, built by middle-class families supporting their own. Network managers, Pritchard suggests, are people who move between different social groups, able to establish broad networks beyond their own social and cultural positions. Using a life-history perspective, the proposition is that the prior experience of particular individuals and groups will make them more, or less, responsive to social interaction across class, gender and culture. This suggests that the propensity for networking is a learned behaviour, and in the next section I explore how a life-history approach can enlighten our understanding of the skills required to develop widening participation in education.

Leadership, biography and working with others

> Despite the powerful and mystifying claims to the contrary, management is a social practice, not a scientific/technological one (Pritchard, 2000, p 48).

In Chapter 3, I spent some time examining the process of change and how management was a joint activity, a collaboration between different participants in any endeavour. In this chapter, I would like to emphasise that leadership should also be seen as a joint activity. Of course, there is a level of coercion in organisations and in certain circumstances workers can find themselves having to get involved in activities that they do not believe in, but when an organisation requires a significant cultural change, coercion will not succeed. In the context of widening participation in education, it is not helpful to think about leaders as those in control, but rather to think about how far those who are being led are prepared to invest in their leader's abilities. To put it another way, without the trust of the group that has to respond to decisions, decisions will not be implemented. Building trust is a social process. It is about how people relate to each other and, as Stacey (2001, p 4) says, 'the culture of an organisation is not something abstract, it is the direct interactions between people.' This means that when we talk about change, management or leadership, we are talking about the relationships and interactions between people and even, at times, their emotions:

> Managing at any time, but more than ever today, is a symbolic activity. It involves energising people, often large numbers of people, to do new things they previously had not thought important. Building a compelling case – to really deliver ... is an emotional process at least as much as it is a rational one (Peters, 1989 p 418).

Investing something of yourself in activities is vital to the success of any project. As Pratt et al (2000, p 67) highlight, '[m]oney, time and communication are commonly recognised as "fuel" [for organisational change]. What is commonly forgotten as a source of energy is people's passion.' In other words, success in making things work is not just about getting things exactly right, since systems are complex and it is unlikely that anyone will ever be able to imagine every eventuality. Rather, success is about a broad-based desire to achieve the goals set. This does not only apply to the leaders of organisations but whole groups of people, as Pratt *et al* (2000, p 67) go on to point out:

> When we talk about engaging people's passion, we are not suggesting working harder or longer. Instead, we suggest it is energising when people are able to work on something they care about, and when they find that others care too.

Leadership is a joint investment between a leader and those who work with her or him. It is an investment of time, energy and commitment. Good leadership will work from mutually agreed principles, things where passion is shared, and, if need be, be built beyond those mutually agreed passions from that firm foundation. People will trust leaders who can demonstrate that there is a good basis for shared understanding but will not trust people whom they feel they do not know and whose world view is alien.

The world of F and HE attracts people who are interested in knowledge development and it is likely that in this environment workers will encounter others who have similar world views. Equally, it is likely that prior experience will have affected their choice of profession (Bagguley, 1992). Few life-history studies have been done to test this, but one study, which examined the life histories of people involved in new social movements, found that it is the intersection of familial socialisation with personal experience or learning which leads to action (Searle-Chatterjee, 1999, p 277). Management theorists have suggested that being more self-aware can improve how managers perform and interact with colleagues. Examining life experiences and personal histories in this way can potentially increase a manager's ability to be more effective.

We all present a particular vision of ourselves in social situations and managers and workers are no different. In any work environment, understanding how these images have developed from prior experience and how they effect our practice can be useful in our future interactions with colleagues and partners. As Morgan (1997, p 26) says:

> All of us operate out of some kind of image of who and what we are. All of us project images, most of which have both negative and positive consequences. If we can come to understand these images, and how they coincide and collide, we have an enormous resource for improving the impact of what we do.

To return to a discussion raised in Chapter 4 in relation to partnership building, while we are generally aware that structures need to be clear and transparent and systems need to be effective and usable, many people are less clear about how to build strong and lasting relationships, and are even more hazy about the effects of interactions. For Morgan, relationships and interactions will be developed in the context of the images that we portray of ourselves. This is the realm of self-identity and it is often either neglected or taken for granted in discussions about managing in F and HE. I suggest that examining the impact of our life experiences can help us understand why we project certain images to others and, as Morgan says: 'By looking in the mirror and confronting our impacts, we have a means of seeing our strengths and understanding our weaknesses (1997, p 37).

This is not fatalistic. I am not proposing that we are only made by past experience. Our life experiences are ongoing and having understood how we project ourselves, we can decide to change the image, as Morgan (1997, p 37) goes on to argue:

> By using the same methods of imagining new roles and new possibilities, we also have an opportunity to re-image and remake ourselves and our behaviours so that our personal and organisational effectiveness can be enhanced on an ongoing basis.

The prior experience of the individuals interviewed for this project did affect the way widening participation developed in their colleges and universities. I am not arguing that only some people can (or will) get involved in widening the student base in education, but the way individuals involve themselves in the process may well be affected by their prior experience. In the following sections, I draw out particular aspects of my interviewees' personalities that seemed to be significantly affecting their practice in widening participation. I highlight four specific areas that were common to many of them: a love of 'place'; political activism; networking and marginality; and the fourth area, where I begin, family and social background.

Family and social background

In some senses, it is hardly surprising that people who are committed to widening participation often come from families where they were the first member of that family to go to a university. Experiencing for themselves the benefits of a university education as opposed to living without one would be likely to encourage individuals to support opportunities to enable others to do the same. The Principal of Northern City College said:

> My dad couldn't read or write throughout his whole life, and in that sense I feel proud to have achieved what I have achieved but I put it down to a bit of luck, being in the right place at the right time (1999).

The Principal of Seaside College also came from a family where HE was not usual:

> I was brought up in a mining village in the Midlands I came from a very ordinary, working-class family where in my primary school, there were 50 kids in my class. That's going back a bit, and only seven passed the 11+. And I think that had a real impact on me. I was one of the lucky seven and I know what education did for me, and it is deeply rooted in me. It can change your life, it can change your perceptions of yourself, it can change your ability to grab opportunities, not just in work terms, but also ... well, no-one in my family had ever been to university before and it was courageous and noble of my parents to support me through that, because I

know how hard it was for them. So, you see it has a more general impact. You see, this is my childhood (1999).

Nevertheless, the issue of family and social background is more complex. Both these people worked in industry before getting involved in education, so have a perspective of the world of work beyond education. Their perspective is not just about others benefiting as they did. Their belief in education is tied directly to their working-class experience. The Principal of Northern City College went on to say:

When I was in industry, I was a shop steward and I learned a lot from that … in industry, you clock in and clock out and you lose pay if you are five minutes late … It is quite different in education … I went to [bad] schools and I had to go back as a adult … In the 60s, there were all these white middle-class kids who used to come and live in the community. They would say to me, 'why have you moved out?' and I would say to them, 'you live in the community because you chose to live in the community, you could chose to live somewhere else, but these people living here can't'. They were usually single men and women but when they got married, they would be off. Let's face it, that used to get me angry. These same people didn't believe in qualifications, and they would say the students don't want them … but these young trendy professionals who talked like that, had all the qualifications you could need. That was something else that got me angry, they had no idea what 'students' wanted. I'd grown up there and I knew the difference it made and so did they but they just pretended. Qualifications give you choice and people do want choice (1999).

The Principal of Seaside College commented:

So coming to this college, particularly, I know, well I don't know first-hand the kind of poverty that people experience here because I didn't come from that desperate a form of poverty that some people experience … but I have enough empathy to know where the facts of deprivation confront real people's lives, and seeing where education can give people that sense of achievement in the face of some of those realities is wonderful (1999).

Their world view creates a very different sense of the purpose of widening participation. It is rooted in a sense that society provides for its members unequally and that equality of opportunity should lie at the heart of any widening participation agenda. For both these principals, choice for people who had not been given choice was the single most important reason for changing practice in their colleges. Widening participation was not about government policy but a deep-seated understanding that education had served one class better than their own and their search for justice in education had driven them to develop alternative strategies in their own organisations.

Several of my interviewees in HE taught in FE or the youth service before going to work in higher education. The Director of the Centre for Continuing Education at Northern University told me:

> I then got a job in FE and worked there a couple of years, went on to work at Luton College of Higher Education, then on to Sheffield City Polytechnic ... I didn't really want to teach full-time students and much preferred teaching part-time students because I find them committed and interested in being there. I suppose it is to do with what they have given up to be able to study. So I started moving more towards that sort of area of work (2000).

Another of the interviewees told me, in relation to her work in access and guidance at Yorkshire University:

> It is about finding out what is going on in the community. The model really is the old community development and detached youth-work model which I was responsible for managing in Derbyshire, so it is not anything new. But it is for HE. The phrase that I use is working with agents for change because I think parents have aspirations and a lot of focus has been around community work for 14-year-olds. And, in my experience, that is too late, as it needs to happen when aspirations are being shaped very early on, in primary schools, and you have to work with parents. Another is working with activists and trade unionists. Those examples of parents, activists and trade unionists highlight that we cannot do it all, and we have to work with people to enable people who have information, to have a grasp of what we do at the university, but most of that I learnt before I began working in the university (1999).

Both these examples demonstrate the role of prior experience outside universities to develop skills in these managers to enable them to take forward the change agenda required for widening participation. It suggests that the conventional training for academics will not necessarily be appropriate for a more diverse HE sector. New skills are needed as the Vice Rector at Capital City University pointed out to me:

> I would say that, for many traditional academics, there is a problem if we widen participation by definition. We have already taken people who may have a longer and sharper trajectory of development. They can reach the same point as an A-level candidate, but the burden of that will fall on people teaching for the first year, and they do not very often want to because they are not trained in it (1999).

Thinking carefully about the range of experiences that colleagues in institutions bring to their work is a vital part of enabling effective change. Life experiences that emphasise different approaches to teaching and learning are important assets in achieving success in widening participation in F and HE. People who have worked in different environments can often look at practice with fresh eyes; in particular, the experience of working with adults returning to education can benefit universities working with younger students who come from groups that are consistently under represented in HE. As Zera and Jupp (1998, p 3) point out, extensive experience was built up over the years in F and AE that proved highly successful in areas such as ABE:

The mass expansion of adult basic education in London under the Inner London Education Authority in the seventies was due, in part, to a co-ordinated network of community educators pounding the streets in search of customers.

This experience still reverberates in the FE sector and some people involved in this work have now moved into HE. Indeed, some of my interviewees learned their practice through their time in FE. It is possible that the reason why my interviewees have been successful in their involvement in widening participation before it became the central feature of government policy is perhaps because of these prior familial and social backgrounds which gave the individuals concerned both the passion and the ability to grasp the issues required to implement success. In the next section, I explore the roots of individuals' passion in more detail by looking at their involvement in political activism.

A commitment to social change

It is hardly surprising that most of the people in management in F and HE at present belong more or less to a similar generation. They are virtually all 'post-war children' who often remember the 1960s either as activists or as children influenced by the social debates of the latter part of the 20th century. Each of my interviewees highlighted the role of political activism as important to their beliefs, their involvement in widening participation and to their practice. When I questioned the heads of continuing education departments in the two old universities studied, they said that politics had, in different ways, influenced their decisions to become involved in widening participation work. The Director of CE at Northern University told me that it was about:

Politics

MS: *Just politics?*

My family background, labour politics. It's about the people I grew up with (2000).

The Head of CE at Midlands University had a different form of commitment. He said, 'I have been involved in Green politics and that has taught me to be more sanguine but it certainly affected my involvement in this work' (2000).

As important as political beliefs being the spark for involvement in the work, others highlighted the skills learned from being involved in political activity. Both my interviewees from Capital City University were enthusiastic about how much they had learned from party activism:

MS: *I am very interested in people's life history. The people I have interviewed are passionate and have got into management as they see this as the only way to create this kind of thing. You actually fell into it?*

I was a strong political activist. I think that training is ideal. All that experience in Labour Party politics leads you to be able to network. I have worked in media for my entire career so there is that sort of lust to communicate. And that need to explain to other people, to tell them what we are about. We do not have a private world. I think because of where we come from, and what we discovered, we are probably more collaborative as an institution than many. I think we are more willing partners (1999).

Equally, the Head of CE at Northern University had similar thoughts:

I think it was very important. I think that in politics sometimes the two go together. Being aware of what the arguments were and being able to persuade and take people with you is crucial. It changed me dramatically because I had been into the preservation of teachers' rights and it changed into the expansion and preservation of the students' rights and sometimes the two conflict. That became difficult at times but I think the political and trade union background was really important, and also it meant that you knew the institutional managers (2000).

They were both concerned to use their influence to see social change. The Rector from Capital City University said:

There were people who believed in the vision, had the vision and want the vision to work. The Vice Rector and I are both historians and spent most of our lives teaching it. It is possible to combine the skills of a historian with this arena. Very few historians can change history! So we get a lot of personal satisfaction from it.

The point is, we first met because of organisation, but I think that neither of us have just relied on being historians as we always have taken the outside view which makes us different, because we are different to others historians (1999).

For the women I interviewed, second-wave feminism was a significant factor. Beginning their working lives during the 1970s, all of them felt that they could imagine a different society because of the strength the feminist movement had given them. The Principal of Capital College responded to a comment I made about her style of management. She put it this way:

I think I'm eclectic, yes ... I'd rather pick up things here and there and go walking with my friends on the moors or whatever and talk it out. I am very much a 'person person' and that is the sort of style that I like to use. I guess I think my background in ABE and feminism has made an impact on how I work now. Overall, I am unhappy with top down approaches. My restructuring was all about removing the top down approach and working in teams. I guess the seventies' battles about human rights, and so on, are still really important to me and from that flows the sort of structures I have tried to create here (2000).

The women managers were very concerned about creativity born out of a sense that conventional approaches to access would not work. The Access and Guidance Co-ordinator from Yorkshire University told me:

It was an odd move into this job. The one consistent feature in my career is work around access and opening opportunities, setting up courses and getting into other interesting areas, moving into progressive and dynamic areas where work is very experimental. Feminism did provide some of that space, so did a lot of my other work. There has always been an attraction to change and times of change, and when I came into this post it was when access and guidance had just been set up, and it's about taking hold of an agenda and taking it somewhere. I have never felt I have to accept things as they are. I do challenge discrimination and I do expect men to be aware (1999).

For these people, their work was not separate from their beliefs. They felt that their careers were rooted in a desire and an ability to make change happen. Most had taken their management positions because they felt they could make a difference and were comfortable with the site of their work, as this middle manager told me:

I am an access sort of person. That is what I want to see achieved. That is why I am comfortable in an institution like this. Maybe I would be better off in one of those hard-nosed elite institutions, but not really, here I can do something I know. The other thing about me is I have worked at a national level as I have the confidence to do that. I used to think that everyone knows better than me, but now I have the confidence because it is right, it is something we have to achieve (Director of CE, Central University, 1999).

Although we are told, and we tell our students, that 'outside' interests are important and should be included in our CVs, seldom do we credit the extent of their importance and value to us as individuals, both in terms of the skills these teach us and in terms of the confidence our beliefs and 'activisms' give us. Further attention should be paid to the role of people's beliefs and activism as factors in how they develop in their careers.

Often with activism comes an appreciation of neighbourhood. Most political activists work in a specific area and come to understand that area and its complexities. Another thread that linked the managers described in this book was their concern about locality.

A sense of place

Widening participation in F and HE, particularly for people from poorer backgrounds, means the availability of locally accessible learning opportunities. It is obvious that limited income means that travel expenses are a disincentive to study. However, simply providing local education is not sufficient. An awareness of locality, the people who live in an area, their interests and the issues that worry them is perhaps more important than simply providing education in their area. This broader awareness will help shape the curriculum offered. It will allow for more appropriate social research with the community and it will alert the lecturers and managers of the F or HE institution to the issues that people in the area are facing when they take on further study. Perhaps most significant of all, if those working in education in the local area are themselves involved in the area, then they have a shared and equal space to relate to others in the community. One of the biggest problems I would identify in community development work is a 'missionary approach' to working in communities. This style of working is often unconscious and is firstly about a set of taken for granted values that are not relevant to the people who live locally. I am not arguing that people have to have experienced living on a council estate, or be black or from a minority community. There are significant differences between communities and, for that matter, social housing estates. Rather, it is about investment in an area, a feeling that you belong and that you have a stake yourself in its development. The Director of Continuing Education at Midlands University drew this point out for me. He said:

> You have an obligation to local area ...

> MS: *And that is the university's vision?*

> Director of CE: Yes, but I think very unevenly achieved. It is a big organisation and some people do not live locally. They live in Oxford, which tells you about where they wish they were, so their commitment to regeneration will be nil. There is also the generation thing ... it is the old lefties that are willing to take part so there is a people issue. As a large corporate player, there is the issue that we have a responsibility to the area. If the area gets worse that means more foreign students might be writing home saying that they have been mugged and have nothing to do. People could say that it is a tip and they wished they went to another university, and so there is a self-interest ... You build up knowledge and trust with local stakeholders and players. That pays off (2000).

For others, it is simply that the place where they work is the city to which they feel a deep sense of commitment:

> The other thing is that I am a Londoner, ingrained Londoner. I was born, went to infant, junior, senior education, college, polytechnic, university in London and now am working in London. So, to me there is a strong commitment to work in this area and doing that work in London, so there is a drive I have about place. London is big and the dynamics are so seductive so it never ceases to fulfil me ... I am part of the same debate about 'can we do things across London together again?'. And I see that prospect exciting (Director of CE, Central University, 1999).

The Principal of Northern City College had worked in several different cities when the post of principal in his home town was advertised. He felt he had to return. He told me:

> I had to come back ... I went to Manchester Poly. When I was there I went to London and did some work and the tutor on the course said I should do more. She said do a postgraduate course, but I came back here. I was concerned about the kids who had dropped out so I set up a stepping stone

between the youth club and traditional FE. I set up a black studies library. The project supported kids who were still in schools, too. Later, of course, as you know, I went back to London, where we worked together but when this job came up, I had to come back. I know the place. My roots are here. I had no choice (1999).

Another faculty member from Northern University felt that he was involved in education because of the area. He said:

I believe that education can transform individuals to make a difference to their community. Why am I in the business for this region? ... I want to see it regenerated. Unemployment is still the norm. It has never recovered. When the miners' strike happened, the men lost everything not just their jobs but their networks, their welfare, everything because it was all connected with the pit and they just went to ground. Hidden miners they're called. They just stayed in. The women were transformed ... mind you, when the strike was over they were told to get back, but they said no ... (2000).

The strength of feeling in these accounts points to the extent to which involvement in widening participation for this generation is an imperative. If harnessed properly, their passion could provide the motor for change that is required. This leads on to the final area of life experience and practice that drew my interviewees together and which seemed significant to their work in the field of widening participation, their role as network managers.

The outsider coming in: networks and marginality (again)

Nearly all my interviewees identified networking as a significant factor in helping them develop change in their organisation. Middle managers highlighted that networking beyond the organisation could keep them in touch with communities outside education, and the experience could even help them to identify the right people with authority within the organisation to implement change. The Access and Guidance Co-ordinator at Yorkshire University told me:

It is a lot to ask of people, and you do not get an idea of strategy unless you have been in a management role. You have not had that experience and it is hard. People who have been in political organisations are people who don't find it so difficult. That's to do with the experience of such organisations (1999).

Others felt that their networks helped them rethink the boundaries of what they did. In thinking about the role of continuing education in widening participation, one middle manager told me that he felt that a network to support CE needed to go beyond those who worked in universities:

At the time, the binary line disappeared, there were important things happening to the polytechnics, indeed the universities as well ...

Continuing education was not a matter for the University to decide because CE happens in different contexts and really if we are serious about building a network then it must be open to people involved, and it can't be exclusive or be within a dominant unit. And that was something that excited me to reach out and work with colleagues within continuing education, and that is what I spend a lot of time doing beyond universities, in colleges and other such environments (Director of CE, Central University, 1999).

Change, in this context, he said, came from working with others beyond university or college walls to provide insights into practice that challenged conventional thinking. Marginality, for him, was an asset that gave him a different perspective from which to view his own institution:

From what we have learned we are moving to a more regional base, in a sense to reflect the changing balance of power and the importance of region, so we are getting involved ... I have enjoyed being involved [in the network] and feel comfortable in it and the values it has. It is a grounding thing for me. It makes me think, 'Is this the right way to do this?', and members of the network can be quite challenging (1999).

Senior managers also saw networking as vital to remaining aware of policy changes, developing new funding streams and being able to introduce new ideas into their organisations. One college principal told me:

Networking is vital, for a whole variety of reasons, especially new ideas, and I'm always looking for other ways to fund the college and its work. If I can see a good idea, we diversify if we can, so that is why we are in on Single Regeneration Budget and today, as an example of networking, I am meeting with someone to discuss funding for another project so I am always on the lookout. I try to use people to help the college grow not only funding but learning, like the open-plan structure of the college. I learned that from a group of architects who did a presentation for me, blew me away really ... so yes, networking and looking out for useful people and ideas (Principal, Capital City College, 2000).

University senior managers also saw the benefit of such contacts:

My Vice Rector's skills have played an important role but it is a question of seizing opportunities. Going back ten years, the odd thing is that the University had hardly any links with the city, they did not want anything to do with us. What we have done is focus the attention of the movers and shakers. By developing those links, we found they got heavily involved in the work and then we got funding and support from them (Rector, Capital City University, 1999).

What comes out of all these comments is that these individuals say they are comfortable with these forms of interaction. They talk about having specific skills and enjoying the work. Often, their skills are developed through activities outside their own work environment and they all saw themselves as being 'people people'. Some saw the marginality of their contacts to their organisation as helpful as it shed light on activity in a different way to internal evaluations. External networks can be a motor for change and can also be useful learning environments for individuals and for their organisations. Most of my interviewees felt they could inhabit more than one world and often felt equally at home with their external networks as within their own institutions. They therefore developed a complex relationship between their organisations and their outside contacts. This sense of marginality, even for senior managers, suggests that change management is significantly about being able to see beyond organisational boundaries and is particularly suited to people who inhabit different worlds.

The effects of personal experience on individual change managers has proved to be significant in this study. I have argued that passion built out of experience creates high levels of commitment, which can benefit organisations and will also provide a successful climate for change. Passion and belief are powerful agents and will inspire colleagues. Equally, an understanding of people who have not accessed education ensures that trust and acceptance are easier to develop. Being rooted in local communities themselves, these managers respond to regeneration activities as activists involved in the process, standing side by side with their neighbours, which limits cultural misunderstandings. If we are to develop new forms of educational provision that will attract different students, many of these skills need to be fostered. It supposes that a new style of management is required. In a changing social and educational climate, we need managers who are comfortable with partnership, with building links between themselves and other different people and groups, as well as managers who can learn from different sites of activity beyond their own institutions.

In the final chapter, I go on to explore some of the factors involved in this changing social and educational environment.

8 Star gazing, futures for widening participation in education

Lots of people do not want their kids to go on studying. It's not just about stimulating access and changing language ... so what do we do, pretend there isn't a problem and send more leaflets out? That is very naive approach and it won't work.

So I think that in terms of managing the process of widening participation, we need to identify and understand what needs to change in us and not just all the perpetual stuff that the potential student is just out there ...

A lot of the constituency that we want to recruit from does suffer from huge under-investment in their education ... You can't just give them an Access course and think that they are going to be fine, if you do, you are living in cloud cuckoo land (Director of CE, Central University, 1999).

This book has described a number of approaches, which have tackled some of the challenges set out in the comments above. Managers can evaluate whether these approaches could apply in their own situation but, as already mentioned, the conditions in which managers in F and HE are able to act is dependent on an overall policy framework provided by governments which, in turn, are shaped by global economic and social forces.

This final chapter looks at some of the social and political influences that will affect the future of F and HE. Some of these influences mitigate against education being more inclusive and participatory, especially if the 'widening' in 'widening participation', is defined in relation to 'stretching' existing resources and practice as both the massification and inclusion forms of widening participation do (Martin, 1999, Thompson, 2000). It is, of course, difficult to predict the future and, although I have called the chapter 'Star gazing', I am not suggesting that either my interviewees or I have clairvoyant powers. Nevertheless, particular outcomes can be predicted from the conditions that are taking hold in the sector. This chapter explores some of these potential futures in education with particular reference to the impact on widening participation. I start by looking at the current position of the sector and attempt to suggest how this climate could develop through the 21st century. I focus on three particular areas of concern: the legacy of competitiveness; the dialogue between recruitment and retention; and, global learning and e-challenges.

Having discussed these challenges, and some suggested outcomes, the chapter goes on to argue for a different approach, a re-conception of the purpose and delivery of post-16 education. I suggest that to deliver learning that is both accessible and appropriate to the needs of different learners, an extensive evaluation of the changing social order is required. Designing a new F and HE approach requires a collaborative engagement between different groups and individuals, not just between educationalists. I do not propose to suggest what this new approach should look like. Indeed, I argue that investigating its parameters is part of the task that faces the sector, but I do suggest a methodology that could be used as a starting point for a more comprehensive and participatory engagement. I begin by arguing that, despite the rhetoric to the contrary, competitiveness is still a significant feature of the landscape of F and HE.

Futures 1: The legacy of competitiveness – mergers and acquisitions

Pritchard (2000) argues that although government policy changed in 1997, the effects of the root-and-branch changes grown out of the 1992 Further and Higher Education Act meant that practice continues to be informed by the ideology of competition. He says (2000, p 48):

> The neo-liberal emphasis on 'individual freedom' provided the basis for a reconstruction of the 'public' as consumers and the public sector as public enterprises engaged in providing services to meet individual consumer/customer/client needs.
>
> The manager became a control figure in public sector reconstruction, charged initially with being responsible and accountable for service provision against centrally controlled 'contract' levels of work.

For many managers in F and HE, this picture will ring as true now as it did during the 1990s. While new money has gone into both F and HE, most of this funding is what is called jam-jar funding or, as Pritchard (2000, 48) puts it, 'being responsible and accountable for service provision against centrally controlled "contract" levels of work'. FE colleges were first to see the effects of competitiveness during the 1990s, and there remain a series of difficulties for FE that spring from that time. One colleague who has worked in refugee education at Capital City College since the 1980s said:

> Well, it is more of the same really. The LSC is just talking about prioritising, which in our business means cuts, again … like last time and the time before. It's the same as the late 1980s, no different, just cuts and scrabbling around for more money (2000).

In other words, while there has been talk about change, and some additional funding, the perception on the ground for project and activity managers is that there is still a struggle to gain funding for work with groups that may not fit the current fashionable categories for widening participation. The problem is that new money usually goes to new projects, developed in partnership and bid for competitively, while much of the work to facilitate widening participation requires stability and sustained involvement. New ideas and new ways of working are necessary in some areas as I have already detailed here, but there is also a substantial body of activity in FE that is difficult to maintain, although the activities would be broadly defined as widening participation work. Stock (1996) points out that prioritising of particular groups' needs in the 1970s was the result of cuts to funding for adult education rather than an expansion of the service. While funding has been increased for widening participation activities in colleges, the effects of prioritising new work has been to cut existing widening participation work in some areas. As the Principal of Capital City College pointed out, some activities are being repackaged as new, when they are simply reinventing older approaches:

> On a more pessimistic note, I wonder if we are not just reinventing the wheel, things that we used to do, happening all over again. For example, in our SRB project, we are taking teachers into people's homes to help them learn in their homes. Do you remember we used to do that 20 years ago? All good stuff but really it should have been sustained if they wanted real results. SRB is fine but it is short term all over again (1999).

The Learning and Skills Council is planning a much more regionally focused provision but the impact on individual colleges is not yet fully known. It is also already clear that difficulties are emerging between the national level of the LSC and its regional arms and between the regional LSCs and their colleges and other providers. The LSC is much more of a planning body than its predecessor, which in itself creates difficulties as managers get used to new relationships. Equally, while regional planning has advantages, for groups whose learning needs are particularly local, regional planning often looks like economies of scale. Of course, learning partnerships do address some of these concerns, but their future is not clear and the focus on strategic partnerships undermines less powerful, neighbourhood and community focused joint work. It is possible to meet the needs of the communities despite core funding, as highlighted by the work at Northern City College, but this requires senior management commitment to find alternative resources.

Mergers between FE colleges are a continuing feature of the landscape of the sector. At its final meeting, the Further Education Funding Council noted that 'rationalisation and college mergers continue to play an important role in the improved financial health of the sector' (FEFC, 2001, p 6). They also commented (p 5) that they expected that it would continue to be a significant feature of FE in the future. It is difficult to predict how the funding regime will develop in further education, but if some of the simplicities of the previous regime remain, risk taking will be limited. Restricting innovation inevitably means that colleges will continue to compete over students who are already in the system, or who are easier to attract.

Collaboration is difficult for colleges when they are competing for the same students. This was an issue for all the colleges studied in this book. The Principal of Seaside College pointed to some of the challenges that this gave colleges:

> At a local level, there are so many different partnerships and co-ordinating what each of them does and preventing duplication is problematic ... really, this collaboration between colleges is key and we haven't got it right yet. In terms of numbers, I am concerned that we haven't yet sorted out how we count students. I actually do not think that it is widening participation if we just recycle students from one college to another (2000).

FE has also been encouraged to diversify into HE activities through partnerships with HE. Participation in HE has levelled off with disastrous consequences for most FE colleges involved in this work. The principals of two of the colleges studied in this book, Seaside and Northern City, had small amounts of HE provision. Neither of these principals saw provision as a major part of their mission, but even here the market for HE work has affected their overall budgets. The sequence of encouragement to diversify and then to retract makes the role of senior management in colleges difficult.

The problem of competitiveness continues to haunt other areas of the sector as well. In an attempt to widen participation, HEIs have been encouraged to apply for funds to increase student numbers. Like FE funding, the bidding process has been developed against a set of criteria which includes partnership working, a notion of new developments and providing courses for under represented groups in HE. This process is, of course, also competitive. Unlike FE, however, any planning to increase numbers is determined at a local level by the university or partnership concerned. Unlike the Learning and Skills Council which now has an explicit planning remit, the HE funding councils remain as funding councils, although increasingly they are aware that elements of a planning approach may be required (HEFCE, 2001b). Seldom does the process of increasing numbers take into account the longevity of widening participation work. The result is an unequal balance between different types of institution where the late application market is becoming harder for universities. New universities and FE colleges are particularly losing out. In other words, in an attempt to increase income, universities have bid for money to increase participation without knowing if they can reach their new targets and in a differentiated market, where some universities are seen to be 'better' than others, market economics prevail:

> If universities are destined to embrace the marketplace, do they understand what forces they are unleashing? It is likely that more vocational subjects, such as business and computing, will prosper, while unpopular subjects – engineering and physics, for example – will die away. The sector is certainly becoming more segmented as the former polytechnics are forced to survive by concentrating on enrolling students from poor, local neighbourhoods and ethnic minorities (Elliot, 2001, p 5).

While there is an increasing realisation that some form of increased planning is required (HEFCE, 2001b), several issues arise from this unplanned market-driven process specifically in relation to widening participation. It suggests that the 'un-planners' have not thought through the distinctions between massification, of which this market-based process is a clear example, inclusion and transformative participation. Government policy favours the inclusion model of widening participation but, in Britain, as in many other developed nations, the legacy of competitiveness and its child, massification, are still dominant. Inclusion takes time, it requires some of the activities that are currently being funded by small grants and short-term money, to work. Most of these projects work with younger children, in early secondary and even primary schools. Recent research suggests that the inclusion model will not produce new students for HE as the 'aspiration raising' initiatives are not attracting students who would not have considered HE in the first place (Utley, 2001). However, even if these activities were to succeed, the results from these projects will not be fully realised for several years. In the meantime, there are additional places available in universities that are not being filled and universities are being penalised for it. The inevitable consequences of this process will ensure that some universities will be unable to sustain their futures and desperate attempts to survive will be introduced. This suggests that mergers across the HE sector can be expected. This process has already started in London but there are other scenarios that may also emerge. Universities that are more powerful may well swallow up smaller HEIs, and HE in FE has a bleak future. For widening participation, which often requires locally available provision, opportunities may shrink, rather than increase, in this market-driven environment. It is also possible that in a competitive environment certain subject areas will become rare while others will be unequally represented across the sector. Several of my interviewees felt this scenario was possible. The Director of Continuing Education at Central University put it this way: 'I think it is heading for more divisions. I think it is going to become even more divided. In some of the things we have talked about before, gaps are going to grow' (2000).

The funding council argues that diversity in the sector is a good thing. However, when the diversity in the sector is not about difference but rather about who has and who has not, it does not serve equity in education. As Brown and Piatt (2001, p 5) point out:

> The effect of all these trends has been to worsen the relative and absolute financial position of certain newer institutions ... certain institutions focusing on widening participation (along with some smaller institutions) are generally in a worse financial position than most older universities.

One of the middle managers interviewed from Midlands University suggested that the future would be based on very clear dividing lines:

> One, the previous Government wanted to privatise education which the present Government has accelerated, which will continue. The process of privatisation ... need not be damaging to widening participation, it changes the strategy. Two there has been a huge diversification within the higher education system ... Because of the old student system, we have been able to rest very heavily on our laurels ... The full-time route is closing up so we can not use that mechanism any more. We have to think

what that means for us. It is very competitive to get in here and even I would find it hard to get in! (1999).

The real legacy of competitiveness is confusion across the sector, as well as a number of mixed messages coming from the funding councils and the Department for Education and Skills. Certainly, there is a need for change in the sector but if we are to prevent a messy, uneven and painful re-alignment of our institutions, government needs to be clear about what it is asking of senior managers. The legacy of competitiveness, unplanned massification, has already proved itself unable to deliver widening participation for many groups of people in society, but it continues and is now threatening the survival of several institutions. The current rhetoric of widening participation focuses on targeting specific groups, which requires planning, which is antithetical to more market driven processes. We need to lay to rest the ghost of competitiveness if we are to succeed in widening participation.

There are considerable challenges offered by the need to both recruit and retain diverse student groups in F and HE, and it is this requirement that lies at the heart of current Government policy. This challenge to the sector is of course correct. It is vital that people, having taken on further study, should be able to complete their study. This relationship between bringing students into study and enabling them to complete it represents a difficulty for the future of F and HE. It lies at the heart of an inclusionist approach to widening participation and is the next concern that I discuss.

Futures 2: The dialogue between recruitment and retention – inclusion in what is

Although access to further study remains an issue, it is now widely accepted that widening participation is as much about retention as it is about access. Retention rates in Britain are generally quite favourably comparable with other countries, but if these rates are broken down between the sectors and the background of the students, it is clear that the picture is more complex. In particular, students who come from lower socio-economic backgrounds and who have fewer qualifications are more likely to drop out or not complete their studies. If widening participation is to mean anything at all, helping students complete their study must be a priority. Many of my interviewees in both further and higher education identified this as their biggest concern. The Principal of Capital City College said:

> I am not asking for special favours here. I want to see our students with good A-levels getting into UCL and Kings ... You see, widening participation for us is not really about getting to people since most of our students are the students the Government tells us we must recruit. It is more about ensuring quality and ensuring success and good results, quality teaching so that students can progress on (1999).

Equally, the issue for HEIs is about completion. The Rector of Capital City University put it this way:

> We need to take on widening participation properly, with real results for
> people, not just saying we can take them in, because they won't stay.
> Widening participation must be linked with improving prospects and this
> is where the role of the academic comes up ... I think that the Government
> needs to recognise that getting a premium on a postcode is like a drop in
> the ocean. You have to do more than that and give people the tools to deal
> with diversity, and we do not have them (1999).

It is becoming increasingly clear that students who have come from diverse
backgrounds do not find the cultures of education easily accessible. If widening
participation is defined as inclusion in what is, as the current Government does,
there is a real need for more funding to provide additional support to enable
those students who see the academic learning process as alien to succeed. Brown
and Piatt succinctly draw out this point when they say (2001, p 3):

> The lower retention rates that are the natural concomitant of
> inadequately funded initiatives for widening access result in institutions
> being financially penalised and having to repay grants. This worsens
> their financial position still further. Yet the Government has instructed
> the Higher Education Funding Council for England to 'bear down on
> non-completion'.

This approach will only increase the pressures already being suffered by those
institutions that attract a wide range of diverse students. Financial pressures on
both F and HEIs and, importantly, on students from poorer backgrounds, create
a spiral of debt and make the possibility of students completing their studies
more difficult. While the review of student finances in Britain addresses some
aspects of these problems, institutions have been told not to 'expect too much
despite their long and costly shopping lists' (Thomson, 2001, p 3). However,
there are other difficulties with an inclusionist approach. Retention is defined in
a time-limited sense, partly because of funding but also because of a vision of
learning that is rooted in what already exists. This model is still based on an
add-on, deficit model of learners. It is rooted in educational practice that is
based on a modernist curriculum, which is perhaps becoming outmoded.
Learning across the lifespan is regarded in some areas as a more useful way of
thinking about F and HE provision. As Jones and Thomas (2001, p 1) point out:
'current government and much institutional thinking focuses on this time-scale
and the associated structures, and attempt to tailor solutions accordingly. Such
an approach seems to assume somewhat narrow ideas of retention, and
progression.'

Widening participation requires a recognition that further and higher
learning may entail alternative qualifications taken over longer, or shorter,
periods of time (Ramsden, 2001). The problem, however, is that the alternative
qualifications that we have are, well, alternative. They do not have the
credibility of the sector, professional bodies or employers. There remains a series
of gold standards in education, the hurdles that you have to clear, A-levels and a
three-year degree, and 'alternative' qualifications are another example of an
add-on approach.

For many of the groups who do not participate in F and HE, employment prospects are an important factor in their decision to study (Woodrow, 2001). Current curricula offered in many areas of the sector do not meet the needs of a changing employment market. Decisions to reject further study may well, for some people, be based on an understandable logic that the investment in the education will not be worth the outcome. The inclusionist approach to widening participation, although emphasising retention, does not question what is offered in F and HE, as Preece (1999, p 13) points out:

> Widening participation [in the learning age] simply means 'anyone who has the capacity for higher education should have the opportunity to benefit from it' (DfEE, 1997, p 49) This implies that HE itself does not need to change. The goal of widening participation, then, is using strategies for inclusion which have only ever succeeded with the already included.

While this comment applies specifically to HE, it could equally apply to FE. Martinez's major study of student achievement (2001) points out that inspiring tutoring and innovative, relevant curricula provide the motivation necessary for students to achieve in college. With an inclusionist approach, if people do not succeed, drop out or change direction, the problem is either with the person concerned or with the lack of add-on support offered; it is not a problem of the way education itself is designed or delivered. This is a serious misconception as the Martinez study suggests. Equally education does not operate in a vacuum, and more attention should be paid to the broader social context for learners as is highlighted from a study of retaining minority student groups at Tower Hamlets College in London:

> Approximately half of the 'minority' students stated that they had wanted to leave their courses at some time during their first year ... this was for a variety of reasons and isolation was one of them ... In relation to isolation, students identified four main groups of experiences: ethnicity in general, religion, language and friendship (Hooper, 2001, p 38).

Hence, in the current conditions in Britain, the rhetoric of widening participation in F and HE does not take account of different experiences in learning and tries to fit people into conventional approaches to knowledge development:

> education policy, funding and qualification awards often reinforce traditional patterns and carry with them unexamined assumptions about smooth transitions and stereotypes of students as 'academic', 'vocational' or 'disaffected'. This can reinforce the view that there are different types of learners who are naturally suited to one pathway, one teaching method, and one qualification which will launch them on the right career path (Gleeson, 2001, p 32).

The future outlined by this scenario suggests that additional add-on funding is what is required to provide for people who do not have the necessary skills to succeed in the present system. A recent survey of FE funding highlighted that an extra £100million would be necessary to resource learning for more 'disadvantaged' learners (Fletcher, 2001). Equally, in HE, there is considerable pressure to increase the five per cent allocated for widening participation to 20 or 25 per cent (Brown and Piatt, 2001). Despite growing pressure for increased funding, this level of funding is unlikely to be simply met from the public purse. Both recruitment and retention are problematic for an inclusionist approach that focuses on adding-on provision and stretching resources in a system that was designed for a different set of criteria and, I would argue, a different age.

There is a growing debate within F and HE that suggests a need for a reconfiguration of diversity of mission. The Director of the Centre for Continuing Education at Central University put it this way:

> Nationally, I think differences between institutions will grow and trying to take the sector as a whole, it will be difficult for us not to leap towards a divide between research institutions and teaching institutions (1999).

Some would argue that additional funding for widening participation attached to certain institutions, which have already demonstrated success in widening access, would be a more appropriate strategy to reach the targets set for F and HE. This approach overturns current strategy, which encourages all institutions to engage in widening participation. An approach that favoured more planned diversity in F and HE could produce a realignment that enabled realistic and culturally sympathetic mergers of institutions, rather than the chaotic scrabble for survival which we are currently beginning to see in the sector.

It is possible that this debate will lead to a more American model of post-sixteen education, which Britain has already examined on several occasions. It will reduce the numbers of both F and HE institutions, creating different configurations of organisation. The requirement from the DfES for the funding council in England to work more closely with the LSC is to be welcomed. However how the plans for 'partnerships for progression' (HEFCE, 2001c) will be worked out from their vague aspirational statements is still to be seen. Some of the Scottish and Welsh models of HE in FE and different sorts of arrangements between HE and FE could be useful to explore.

In some cases, a blurring between F and HE would create a specific focus on widening participation. However, that could leave the door open for other institutions to either focus on providing 'elite higher education' or focus on providing the students who would attend the elite HEIs, in other words elite 'schools'. In this model, it is possible that stand-alone FE could find itself driven down a route that emphasises coercion into learning for the excluded, especially programmes that emphasise skills for employment (Field, 2000). This would, of course, shape the nature of the curriculum still further in institutions that focus on widening participation. While several of my interviewees saw this scenario as one definite possibility, none felt it would benefit the cause of widening participation significantly. Providing more money for widening participation is attractive and, to some in a few institutions, separating off an elite higher education is attractive, but my interviewees felt that the real people to lose out in this scenario would be those who are currently most excluded from education. The fundamentals of the education map would remain the same and, while more people from poorer backgrounds may well have some level of access to further and higher level study, the outcomes for these groups would remain unequal. Elite institutions would set gold standards for employment and inequality in society would continue to be exacerbated. As in the US, the gold standards, unequal status and, despite a promise of more money, unequal resourcing would remain.

So far, we have only considered issues that relate specifically to the conditions present within British society. However, as I pointed out in Chapter 2, post-16 education, as all other areas of social policy, is part of a global redefinition of society and these forces will affect the future of the sector. Field (2000, p 111) emphasises that 'in most Western countries, welfare state provision is being reformed in order to transfer responsibility away from the government towards the individual.' Increasingly, the onus is on individuals having to take risks with their life decisions, risks that previously had been borne by governments. It is to those global forces and their impact on the future of widening participation that I now turn.

Global learning and e-challenges

There is a sort of knee-jerk reaction when new technologies are mentioned in relation to development. They are, like education, seen as one of the keys to success in the 21st century. As Field (2000, p 17) points out: 'Hardly a single policy paper emerges from the European Commission on education and training ... that does not refer to the need to build a European information society.'

Certainly, new technologies have become a significant feature of our society in the 21st century. In the context of FE, there are difficulties with new technologies and access as the Principal of Capital City College pointed out:

> I mean, some people think it is all going to be virtual, or whatever.
> Certainly, there is a massive need for the staff in further education to get
> access, never mind the students. We are working on it here. We want better
> IT communications and are developing it, but, at present, only about 20
> per cent of our teaching staff have access to computers so in our
> communications, there are real gaps. We simply can't afford to pay for this
> (1999).

It is difficult to see how colleges are expected to equip their students if the staff themselves do not have proper access. The problem for widening participation in some parts of FE is that students may well be being limited in their learning as there is no infrastructure to deliver new curriculum developments in new technologies. As Field (2000, p 17) points out: '[The question is one of] who really has access to the new ICTs and who has at best only restricted and partial access: citizenship of the information society is conditional upon the availability of the technologies.'

The market for education is increasingly much more global. In searching the World Wide Web, it is possible to find a range of learning materials from eminent colleges and universities such as MIT and Harvard Business School.

However, this form of learning in itself did not seem to worry my interviewees. The Rector of Capital City University put it this way:

> Well, I do not share most of the worries of some others concerning IT and that we will all be put out of a job. I do not see that as there are demands for navigation, guiding people to learn from the knowledge available and a great deal of that has to be done page to page rather than simply electronically. So, I do not share the view that you can simply teach over the Internet because people want a great deal of direction. The fact is, there are new ways of using different technologies for research so we both know what technology offers, and we all agree it can be used for a resource, but people will always require networking, guidance, confidence building ... (1999).

Here, he is pointing to the recognition that learning is a social process. In the context of widening participation, this is perhaps even more important where students from diverse backgrounds will need to engage in a dialogue with tutors about their learning and will need to build, as the Rector identified, 'confidence'. The potential of e-learning will benefit those who already have the confidence and experience of prior learning. In other words 'the most reluctant learners, and the most excluded and peripheral groups ... are unlikely to embrace learning through ICTs' (Field, 2000, p 99).

As the corporate plan for the Learning and Skills Council (2001, p 3) points out:

> While the information revolution brings benefits for the majority, it carries great risks for those left on the margin ... The estimated one in five adults in Britain who cannot function effectively with written words or numbers are more than ever excluded from our fast moving society.

The excitement about the future of learning in an electronic age should, therefore, be tempered by the evidence that it may in fact create greater divides between groups.

It is impossible to deny that new forms of communication have affected the way societies, such as Britain, are developing. There is a serious concern; especially if the scenario painted above develops. Educational provision will be more focused on consumer need and become more discriminatory rather than less. Equally important to this new form of consumerism for education is the kind of training and learning that students will need in this new communications-based society. The Rector went on to say:

> Also what comes out the other end is changing, the kind of jobs that are available. I see a growth in independent working. I do not think the corporates are soaking up the kind of labour force that education is producing and, in addition, if you think about where people like to live and work they may choose to do something different in order to stay where they are. We need to be part of that process too. So I think the university will be different. Universities may need to be bigger than they are (1999).

Ramsden (2001) suggests that mergers will accelerate in higher education to 'make the best use of resources, and especially to minimise overhead costs' (p 89). He proposes that the increase in mergers will produce larger institutions that will be more successful in a global market. However there is no real evidence that this process will in itself support the cause of widening participation further, especially if the issue of retaining students from poorer backgrounds is examined in more detail.

In reality, it is likely that the outcome of these challenges for the sector will be some sort of mix between continued, unplanned massification and mergers and a more structured diversity of mission across the sectors, drawing further and some elements of higher education closer together in some instances, and creating a more elite system in others.

While it is very difficult to predict how education will develop, it is clear that society is shifting significantly. Many of the global educational policy statements highlight the need for what they call lifelong learning. Lifelong learning, like widening participation, has different meanings. For many, lifelong learning offers a solution to the need for continual skill updating because of the speed of change in knowledge acquisition. It will enable learning that refocuses from outmoded practices to new ways of working, providing employees who can adapt without difficulty. This process has significant implications for widening participation. Indeed, a large part of the rationale for widening participation has been because of these global economic pressures to refocus post-industrial societies into making their workforces competitive and responsive to new economic conditions. In other words, new forms of inequality emerge. For those that have, more is given, and for those that have not, more is taken away. But, as Beck (1996) points out, the responsibility for developing the resources to succeed lies with the individual. It is they who bear the risk.

I have argued that a market-place model of post-16 education is counter-productive to widening participation. I have also argued that widening participation as inclusion in what already exists may not be sufficient for the needs of new learners and also, that it may be that the curricula offered in the sector will not be able to meet the needs of our future society, nor tackle the inequalities that this society throws up. For me, 'universities [and FE colleges, schools, educational curricula] ... have been too narrow' (Rector, Capital City University, 1999). Griffin (1999, p 14) neatly draws together these concerns and sets out a series of challenges that need to be addressed for education:

> What is happening to systems, authorities and compliance mechanisms in postmodern conditions? ... What are the implications of the breaking down of the old distinctions between education and work, or education and leisure, or between the sectors of the education system, or between the various sites where people learn? What are the implications of de-industrialisation, of the fragmentation of social and cultural life, or of the sovereignty of the consumer and the market in education?

The final section of this chapter, rather rashly, attempts to address some of his questions.

Developing new knowledge, struggling towards transformative participation

As I have consistently argued throughout this book, widening participation is not one type of activity, and this has created confusion about the direction necessary for change. For example, at an immediate level, the British government target to shift from 30 to 50 per cent of under-30-year-olds achieving some form of HE by 2010 is clear, but what is not clear is how to achieve this or how realistic it is in the current climate. Achieving the government's targets, whether the HE targets or the NVQ targets of FE, will require re-examining curriculum design, developing more diverse recruitment strategies and a more seamless educational provision where different sectors are more permeable. Some of these activities are already underway. F and HE work closely together in many situations. HE 'aspiration raising' partnerships with schools are now common place. New forms of curriculum especially, but not exclusively, in FE are increasingly seen as a necessary shift to meet the needs of new workers. However, these may well not be sufficient. More serious questions need to be asked about the nature of what education should do in our society.

The current prevailing wisdom in both Britain and other OECD countries highlights the role of education in developing skills for the changing world of work and as a major contributor to social cohesion. Less discussed is the potential of education to support social development. In a risk society, some groups find negotiating their futures difficult. A model of education that contributes to the process of social development offers an opportunity for groups that have had few of the benefits of society to engage in affecting change. It is not only about increasing the numbers of people in learning or including groups who have historically always been left out of education but it is about transforming the way people participate and thereby transforming the educational institutions themselves.

Boundaries that were clear between nations are dissolving. Some nation states, which seemed so fixed in the latter half of the 20th century, have be swept away. Distinctions between work and home are less marked and employment patterns are more blurred. In this climate, a new educational order is beginning to be established (Field, 2000). Knowledge transition and knowledge creation will need to be developed in more diverse and creative ways, and students at all levels will need to be more engaged and active in the process than is currently the case (Edwards, 1997). This is not about a deficit model of providing more support or about improving (or lowering) standards. It is about overhauling what Freire (1972) called a 'banking system of education', where knowledge is stored up and learners become receptacles to 'fill' with knowledge. A new education must develop critical citizens who are not only active in their communities and in work, but who, also, are able to contribute to the changing nature of society.

I have already noted in Chapter 2 that Edwards (1997) argues that this more radical notion of widening participation is quite marginal and not very powerful in the discourse, and indeed I expect this will remain the case.

However, the thinking behind this approach and its methodology, which I develop further here, may be useful to enabling a more developmental education system than the 'narrow' system that has been in place. As Usher *et al* (1997, p 190) point out, 'alternative and more marginalised approaches ... which, despite their often oppositional and powerless status, may none the less be more appropriate'. This is what I call transformative participation.

The idea for a transformative participation in education grew out of work developed in the 'south' has been transferred and adapted in the 'north' (Chambers, 1999, p 3), especially from a methodology called Participatory Rapid Appraisal (PRA). The key principals of PRA are that local solutions to issues of poverty develop from local people, who have expert knowledge of their area, working with academics to design solutions. As Chambers (1999, p 1) puts it, PRA is a:

> growing family of approaches, methods and behaviours to enable people to share, enhance and analyse their knowledge of life and conditions, and to plan, act, and monitor and evaluate.

Most of the work done in PRA relates to development of localities and the facilities for those localities but, increasingly, it has been suggested that PRA approaches could be used to transform institutional practices. In the context of widening participation this would suggest that it is not about including more people into already-existing institutions or providing a set of skills that will make people more employable. Rather, what PRA could offer would be an approach that draws together local people, excluded people, if you like, and academics to examine issues of relevance to their lives. In this sense, it is akin to the ideas surrounding the 19th-century working-class notion of 'really useful knowledge', as defined by Johnston (1979) because the engagement in a PRA approach is directed at real-life experience. The solutions can be seen to have a direct impact on conditions.

Like some of the more recent work growing out of the social purpose tradition (Johnston, 1999; Usher *et al*, 1997), PRA methodology has learned to be critical of the romaticisation of community (Guijt and Shah, 1998). It is possible to combine elements of the social purpose tradition with the experience of PRA to create a different way of working with groups and communities. This requires a 're-theorising of community' to 'reconnect the private lives of individuals with their public lives as citizens' (Crowther *et al*, 2000, p 178), and it can, and must, work across the age range. As well as theorising it requires changes in practice and behaviour. This is where PRA has particular value. It offers practitioners methods and approaches that they should adopt in work with different groups. According to Chambers (1999, p 10) behaviours common to PRA include approaches such as:

> they do it ... local people ... as investigators and researchers ... beyond this, their own analysis ... [using methods such as] time lines and trend and change analysis ... listing major remembered local events ... people's accounts of the past ... changes in land use ... and the causes of changes and trends.

This approach does not only offer solutions for community development learning but could be adapted for a variety of settings including part-time work-based learning which may well contribute to the achievement of government targets for widening participation. If education has power, it must be that it can give people the tools for knowledge development. The methodology used to develop these basics could draw on collaborative inquiry and PRA approaches. It is to the need for the development of such 'basics' to enable widening participation, that I now turn.

Learning across the lifespan, developing new curricula, new literacies

Further and higher education do not exist in a vacuum, and widening participation must be considered in the context of our overall educational structures. In other words, I am suggesting that for widening participation to develop, initial education needs to be transformed first. It is surprising that, so far, government has not really addressed the issue of school education, but, as Field (2000, p 139) argues, if the new educational order is to succeed, it needs to deliver a new learning curriculum that includes the basics, whatever they are. Current policies for schools, as Field points out, are based on maintaining an old-fashioned set of standards dominated by a collection of measures that judge success or failure through 'effectiveness' but, as Fielding (2000) notes, school effectiveness policies are too functional to develop all aspects of the students. He says (2000, p 413):

> Its thin, measurement driven notion of schooling too easily marginalizes concerns for wider, more profound aspirations for the development of persons; and education itself is refashioned in ways which make the call for community seem weak, undemanding and vague.

School education therefore needs to rethink how it offers young people the tools for personal and social development. I suggest that a new curriculum that is developed around the idea of 'literacies' could offer the beginnings of widening participation. I do not mean reading and writing or learning languages, although the basics must include these, but rather a broader set of literacies that enable people to negotiate their own futures. These will also include a literacy of number, of new technology, a science literacy, research literacies and cultural literacies. In all of these, the learner would be developing the language of questioning, to seek out new ways of understanding our world, or 'learning how to learn' (Field, 2000, p 136). These 'basics' will sometimes be acquired at a young age, but should be developed throughout life. Beyond initial learning, the role of widening participation needs to be focused on a vision of lifelong learning that does not see the three-year undergraduate degree as the only goal of further or higher study, but rather recognises that learning will need to be continuous. Of course, for some, taking the three-year undergraduate degree while studying full-time is appropriate, but for many, further- and higher-level learning will become more appropriate as they develop in their careers or through other life changes. Learning in the workplace or the community will need to grow and be cemented in the sector, and here the methodologies used in PRA could be more useful than many conventional approaches used in F or HE. This will require a new approach to qualifications, as Field (2000, p 144) suggests:

> Rather than identifying the institutional context and programme in which teaching has taken place, there is a need for qualifications that reflect the learning gain that has taken place.

For managers in the sector, a transformative approach to widening participation will produce a distinctive agenda for change. At an operational and institutional level, a dialogue with teacher educators and with researchers needs to begin to examine urgently the initial education curriculum and learning approach. Beyond the institution, taking this approach suggests a closer identification and connection with locality. It requires managers to develop work practices that take for granted links between academics, students, employers and community members. It suggests new alliances with initial education in the locality, to develop research for greater participation at school level and to create a permeable approach to education across sectors. It requires the establishment of communication systems within and beyond institutions that are multi-faceted and allow for feedback that can affect change in organisations and in learning. Practitioner experience with communities needs to be drawn together with researchers and the techniques of engagement need to ensure that people whom the institution is targeting are involved in the development of learning opportunities and experiences. Increasingly, managers will need to work beyond their institutions and outside their locality at a national and international level.

At a national and strategic level, the agenda should focus on curricula, qualifications and an ongoing political engagement to address student poverty in all its forms. In particular, beyond the debate about fees for full-time degrees, and the inequalities of loans, the needs of part-time students, in both F and HE, will need further consideration. Managers need to take forward discussions on appropriate and acceptable qualifications that take account of diversity in learners, new knowledge development and recognition that learning sites are not always connected with traditional educational establishments. This debate needs to include professional bodies and employers – who are often more conventional than academics. This approach also suggests that we need to rethink the idea of what curricula are, what assessment is required and to what extent that assessment needs to be based on bullet-point criteria rather than themes, theories and issues. It presupposes that education need not be hierarchical and that learning can, and should, take place in very different sites.

At an international level, education managers need to continue to examine other education systems and develop the dialogue with academics and other interested groups about the nature of further and higher learning in the context of our changing social order. Increasingly, communities of interest as well as local communities will have a significant role to play in the development of this new approach, as Field (2000, p 149) reminds us:

> social relationships can and do also take root over distances of time and space. New technologies are starting to play quite a spectacular role in bringing communities of interest ... as well as communities of practice ... across barriers of space and time that were previously seldom, if at all, passable.

In this book, I have set out a number of different approaches to widening participation many of which draw on ideas of transformative participation within current circumstances. The research partnerships between FE and Midlands University, the associate student scheme at Central University, the development of news ways of working at Capital City College, the DISCs and the local partnerships in Northern City College all have elements of transformative participation. Each shows how engagements between different people who share objectives will act as catalysts for innovations.

Transformative participation will not only affect practice but will affect the people who participate, as the Principal of Northern City College points out:

> Because they [my ex-students] are now saying, 'hang on a second, what are you doing to my child?' and so on, 'I have now got enough knowledge to challenge.'
>
> Education does that ... I meet guys at football, and they're on some of our programmes and they say, 'I'm talking to the telly, "you can't say that"', they're challenging the telly, the current affairs programmes, that's what education is about ... you question, you question, because academics and all those who are in the field, that's what its about, they continually question. 'Hang on a second ... is that the case?, let me test it', and that's legitimate ... but for many working class people they don't feel that they have the right to challenge the government, but education can change that (1999).

The students have developed the confidence to challenge authority's right to question their own and their family's experience. They no longer accept 'facts' but challenge the way information is disseminated. The learning approach, which he is describing, is not one that suggests 'right' answers but is concerned with inquiry and research, like PRA, it is about behaviours where 'they do it'. This is a very novel approach to education, as Desforges (2000, p 8) highlights: 'The models of learning implicit in [conventional] practice are largely based on knowledge transmission, theories entirely at odds with contemporary understandings of learning.'

Knowledge that is developed in educational establishments is not universal knowledge; the whole edifice of education is based on fashions of discourse, threads of conversations that excited groups of researchers. We need to question who makes knowledge and suggest that our truth making in education is only one way of talking about material conditions. As Edwards (1998, p 108) points out: 'Poststructuralist and postmodern approaches would result in a reflexive interrogation of how knowledge is transmitted rather than the transmission of a body of knowledge.'

There are clearly lessons that can be learned from earlier models of social purpose education but the material conditions in which we now work are not the same as those of the 1960s. As Griffin (1999, p 14) says, we have to take account of the extent of the 'fragmentation of social [economic] and cultural life'. We need to look to the development of new forms of learning alliances, some of which will be welfarist, some capitalist and some more diffuse in intent. Our education systems and institutions were designed to meet the needs of modernity/capitalism. They focused on learning within specified institutions whose identities were taken from the age range of their learners. Much of the education that was offered related to becoming socialised for a job for life, at whatever level students were certified to operate. Given the changes in our social order, whatever term we choose to give it – the growth in flexible working, the transformation of communications and diversity of work patterns and work premises – is it not time to investigate a solution more radical than attempting to include people in what already exists?

Creating a new agenda for transformative participation that addresses our changing social needs is challenging but, I believe, possible. Surely, by drawing together different groups of people – researchers, educationalists and community members – to investigate learning and social development we can create curricula that are useful and rigorous to support a diverse society and a changing economic climate.

Placing resources and effort into such research will produce results that could create a very challenging and different way of organising education and a very different set of practices that enable learning. It is an exciting prospect to develop a research-driven education system that is not obviously stratified by age or simplistic notions of level or confined to specific institutions. Learning could develop a sense of itself as a mutual process of development to create new knowledges that transform our social lives.

Working together for transformative participation may well produce new forms of organisation, some of which will be new learning environments. It does not pre-suppose that planning in this changing society is easy or as simple a process as it was in the era of welfarism, but this approach does suggest a way of dealing with the shifting boundaries and increasingly ubiquitous nature of knowledge development. It takes change for granted and suggests an approach to management that relies on co-evolutionary partnerships. This approach to learning is beginning to gain ground, as illustrated by Desforges' comments (2001, p 9):

> This strategy, flowing from modern learning theory, calls for new partnerships between researchers, tutors and teachers, students and college managers, with a shared commitment to transforming the process at the heart of education – the process of learning. It would be necessary to develop management tools, assessment instruments, a lively curriculum, and a set of basic principles operationalised in practice in pursuit of high-powered learning – and to develop their use through research-based practice.

There is urgency for this work to take hold. The crisis across both sectors is deepening and managers in post-16 education need to be alive to opportunities and development. Rethinking who we are as educationalists and what we do is not just an intellectual exercise but is vital to the development of our futures. As the Rector of Capital City University said:

> We just have to be willing to change as we go along. That way whatever the decision at the end, we will already be pointing in that direction. We have to be able to move quickly and time is not on our side (1999).

References

Action on Access (2001) 'Partnerships to Widen Participation in Higher Education Ideas for Effective Collaboration', online at: http://www.brad.ac.uk/admin/conted/action/GPG/gpguide.htm

Adams, M. (2001) 'Changing the Culture: Addressing the Needs of Disabled Students', *Update on Inclusion: Widening Participation in Higher Education*, 3, Spring, 17–18.

Adizes, I. (1992) *Mastering Change: The Power of Mutual Trust and Respect in Personal Life, Family Life, Business and Society*, California: Adizes Institute Publications.

Advisory Group on Citizenship (Crick Report) (1998) *Education for Citizenship and the Teaching of Democracy in Schools Final Report*, London: QCA.

Arblaster, L., Conway, J., Foreman, A. and Hawtin, J. (1995) *Asking the Impossible? Inter-agency Working to Address the Housing, Health and Social Care Needs of People in Ordinary Housing*, London: Jessica Kingsley.

Atweh, B. and Bland, D. (1999) 'Beyond Access and Participation Towards Social Justice – The SARUA Project Queensland University of Technology Australia', *Widening Participation and Lifelong Learning: The Journal of The Institute for Access Studies and The European Access Network*, 1, April, 27–34.

Bagguley, P. (1992) 'Social Change, The Middle Classes and the Emergence of "New Social Movements": A Critical Analysis', *The Sociological Review*, 40, 26–48.

Bass, B. M. (1981) *Handbook of Leadership: A Survey of Theory and Research*, London: The Free Press.

Beck, U. (1992) *The Risk Society*, London: Sage.

Blunkett, D. (2000) 'We Are Making A Difference', *The Guardian*, 3 November.

Bourdieu, P. (1984) *Distinction: A Social Critique of the Judgement of Taste*, Cambridge, MA: Harvard University Press.

Brown, R. and Piatt, W. (2001) *Funding Widening Participation in Higher Education: A Discussion Paper*, London: Council for Industry and Higher Education.

Bynner, J. and Egerton, M. (2001) *The Wider Benefits of Higher Education, Report by the Institute of Education, University of London sponsored by HEFCE and the Smith Institute*, Bristol: HEFCE.

Calman, K. C. (1994) 'Working Together, Teamwork', *Journal of Interprofessional Care*, (8) 1, 94–103.

Chambers, R. (1999) 'Relaxed and Participatory Appraisal: Notes on Practical Approaches and Methods', online at: www.ids.ac.uk

Coare, P. (2000) *Adult Exclusion Sussex: A Research Report*, Brighton: University of Sussex, Centre for Continuing Education.

Coleman, G. (1991) *Investigating Organisations A Feminist Approach*, Bristol: SAUS.

Coleman, J. (1994) *Foundations of Social Theory*, Cambridge, MA: Belknap Press.

Crowther, J, Martin, I. and Shaw, M. (2000) 'Turning the Discourse', in Thompson, J (ed), *Stretching the Academy The Politics and Practice of Widening Participation in Higher Education*, Leicester: NIACE.

Dearing, R. (1997) *Higher Education in the Learning Society*, London: National Committee of Inquiry into Higher Education.

Delmar, R. (1986) 'What is Feminism?', in Mitchell, J. and Oakley, A. (eds), *What is Feminism*, Oxford: Blackwell.

Desforges, C. (2000) 'Research Agendas: Towards Increasing Student Achievement', *College Research: A Journal for FE and Lifelong Learning*, (3) 1, Summer, 7–9.

DfEE (1998) *The Learning Age: A Renaissance for a New Britain*, Sheffield: Department for Education and Employment.

DfEE (1999a) *Learning to Succeed: A New Framework for Post-16 Learning*, Sheffield: Department for Education and Employment.

DfEE (1999b) *Lifelong Learning Partnerships Remit*, January, online at: http://www.dfee.gov.uk/llp/remit.htm

DfEE (2000) *The Excellence Challenge: The Government's Proposals for Widening the Participation of Young People in HE*, Nottingham: Department for Education and Employment.

Duke, C. (1994) 'Funded Research and the Management of Innovation', *Studies in the Education of Adults*, (26) 2, October, 219–35.

Duncan, N. (ed) (1996) *Body Space: Destabilising Geographies of Gender and Sexuality*, London: Routledge.

Duncan, P. and Thomas, S. (2001) *Evaluation of Community Champions and Community Development Learning Fund*, (280) July, Sheffield: Department for Education and Skills.

Edwards, R. (1998) 'Quality, Relevance and Scholarly Writing Open University', *Studies in the Education of Adults*, (30) 2, October, 105–09.

Edwards, R. (2000) 'Lifelong Learning, Lifelong Learning, Lifelong Learning: A Recurrent Education?', in Field, J. and Leicester, M. (eds), *Lifelong Learning: Education Across the Lifespan*, London: Routledge/Falmer.

Edwards, R. and Miller, N. (2000) 'Inclusion and the Denial of Difference in the Education of Adults', in Jackson, A. and Jones, D. (eds), *Researching Inclusion: Papers from the 30th Annual Conference of the Standing Conference on University Teaching and Research in the Education of Adults*, University of Nottingham in conjunction with SCRUTREA: Continuing Education Press, 14–26.

Elliot, Major L. (2001) 'It's Your Call', *The Guardian*, 14 August, 4–5.

FEFC (2001) *Council News*, (64) March, NEWS/1246/01, Coventry: FEFC.

Feyerabend, P. (1975) *Against Method*, London: New Left Books.

Field, J. (1999) 'Participation Under the Magnifying Glass', *Adults Learning*, (11) 3, November, 10–14.

Field, J. (2000) *Lifelong Learning and the New Educational Order*, London: Trentham Books.

Fletcher, M. (2001) *The Costs of Disadvantage*, London: Learning and Skills Development Agency.

Flude, R. (1999) 'Building a Framework', *Adults Learning*, (10) 8, April, 16–17.

Forrester, K. (1995) 'Learning in Working Life: The Contribution of the Trade Unions', in Mayo, M. and Thompson, J. (eds), *Adult Learning Critical Intelligence and Social Change*, Leicester: NIACE.

Francis, D. H. (1989) 'Socio-economic and Cultural Problems of Declining Industrial Regions: The Case of South Wales Valleys', in Alheit, P. and Francis, H. (eds), *Adult Education in Changing Industrial Regions* Verlag Arbeiter-Bewegung und Gesellschaftswissenschaft.

Fraser, L. (1999) 'Widening Participation through Pre-entry Guidance for Adults', *Update on Inclusion: Widening Participation in Higher Education*, (1) 1, Spring, 15–17.

Freire, P. (1972) *The Pedagogy of the Oppressed*, Harmondsworth: Penguin.

Fryer, R. H. (1997) *Learning for the Twenty-first Century. First Report of the National Advisory Group for Continuing Education and Lifelong Learning*, London: NAGCELL.

Gallacher, J. and Thomson, C. (1999) 'Further Education: Overlapping or Overstepping', *Scottish Journal of Adult and Continuing Education*, 5 (1), 9–24.

Giddens, A. (1990) *The Consequences of Modernity* Cambridge: Polity.

Gleeson, D. (2001) 'Transforming Learning Cultures in FE', *College Research: A Journal for FE and Lifelong Learning*, (4) 3, Summer, 30–33.

Gravatt, J. (2000) 'The Disappearing Act', *College Manager*, March, 34–36.

Griffin, C. (1999) 'Lifelong Learning and Social Democracy', paper presented at the University of Sussex Continuing Education Forum, Summer, 1–15.

Halsey, A. H. (1972) *Educational Priority: Problems and Policies*, London: The Stationery Office.

Harper, H. (1997) *Management in Further Education: Theory and Practice*, London: David Fulton.

Hawkins, P. and Winter, J. (1997) *Mastering Change – Learning the Lessons of the Enterprise in Higher Education Initiative Higher Education and Employment*, Sheffield: DfEE.

HEFCE (2001a) *Strategies for Widening Participation in Higher Education. A Guide to Good Practice*, Bristol: HEFCE.

HEFCE (2001b) *Supply and Demand in Higher Education*, Bristol: HEFCE.

HEFCE (2001c) *Partnerships for Progression. Proposals by the HEFCE and the Learning and Skills Council*, Bristol: HEFCE/Learning and Skills Council.

Hooper, I. (2001) 'Retaining and Supporting "Minority" Students in Tower Hamlets College', *College Research: A Journal for Further Education and Lifelong Learning*, (4) 3, Summer, 36–39.

Hornby, S. (1993) *Collaborative Care: Interprofessional, Interagency, and Interpersonal*, Oxford: Blackwell.

Houghton, A. (1998) 'Extending the Guidance Boundaries: An Exploration of Educative and Empowering Guidance Strategies for Learners Who Have Been Long-term Unemployed', in Preece, J., Weatherald, C. and Woodrow, M. (eds), *Beyond the Boundaries: Exploring the Potential of Widening Provision in Higher Education*, Leicester: NIACE.

Hudson, B. (1987) 'Collaboration in Social Welfare: A Framework for Analysis', *Policy and Politics*, (15) 3, 175–82.

Johnston, R. (1999) 'Adult Learning for Citizenship: Towards a Reconstruction of the Social Purpose Tradition', *International Journal of Lifelong Learning*, (18) 3, May–June, 175–90.

Johnston, R. and Croft, F. (1998) 'Mind the Gap: Widening Provision, Guidance and Cultural Change in Higher Education', in Preece, J., Weatherald, C. and Woodrow, M. (eds), *Beyond the Boundaries: Exploring the Potential of Widening Provision in Higher Education*, Leicester: NIACE.

Jones, R. and Thomas, L. (2001) 'Not Just Passing Through: Making Retention Work for Present and Future Learners', *Widening Participation and Lifelong Learning*, 3 (2), 1–4.

Kennedy, H. (1997) *Learning Works: Widening Participation in Further Education*, Coventry: Further Education Funding Council.

King, C. (1995) 'Making It Happen – Reflections on a Varied Career', in Slowey, M (ed), *Implementing Change From Within Universities and Colleges: 10 Personal Accounts*, London: Kogan Page.

Kneale, S. J. (1994) 'Discrimination – A Hidden Barrier to the Development of Interprofessional Practice', *Journal of Interprofessional Care*, (8) 2, 150–72.

Layer, G. (1995) 'Student Guidance and Support – Changing the Approach', in Slowey, M. (ed), *Implementing Change From Within Universities and Colleges: 10 Personal Accounts*, London: Kogan Page.

Layer, G. (2001a) *Building on Previous Experience?*, draft paper for Action on Access.

Layer, G. (2001b) 'Widening Participation – So What, Why and How?', *Educational Developments*, SEEDA, 2, February, 10–12.

Learning and Skills Council (2001) 'The Learning and Skills Council Draft Corporate Plan', online at: http://www.lsc.gov.uk/

Lifelong Learning Partnerships (2000) 'Role of Learning Partnerships', online at: www.lifelonglearning.co.uk

Loxley, A. (1996) *Collaboration in Health and Welfare: Working with Difference*, London: Jessica Kingsley.

Lyotard, J.-F. (1984) *The Post Modern Condition: A Report on Knowledge* Manchester: Manchester University Press.

Martin, I. (1999) 'Lifelong learning for Democracy: Stretching the Discourse of Citizenship', *Scottish Journal of Adult and Continuing Education*, (5) 2, 89–104.

Martinez, P. (2001) *College Improvement: The Voice of Teachers and Managers*, Learning and Skills Development Agency, online at: www.lsagency.org.uk

McGivney, V. (1992) *Motivating Unemployed Adults to Undertake Education and Training*, Leicester: NIACE.

Megson, C. (1999) 'Strategic Partnerships. Making Learning Work for Staffordshire', *Widening Participation and Lifelong Learning: The Journal of the Institute for Access Studies and The European Access Network*, (1) 1, April, 41–42.

Morgan, A. (2001) 'Some Paradoxes in Participation', *The Times Higher Education Supplement*, December.

Morgan, G. (1997) *Imagin.I.zation: New Mindsets for Seeing, Organizing and Managing*, London: Sage.

Morris, A. (2000) 'New Look, New Ideas', *College Research: A Journal for Further Education and Lifelong Learning*, (3) 1, 4–5.

National Taskforce for Widening Participation (2000) *Ideas for Inclusion: An A to Z for Practitioners*, London: HEFCE.

NIACE (1993) *An Adult Higher Education: A Vision*, Leicester: NIACE.

Organisation for Economic Co-operation and Development (OECD) (1996) *Lifelong Learning for All*, Paris: OECD.

Payne, J. (1999) 'Perspectives on Lifelong Learning', *Adults Learning*, (10) 8, April, 9–12.

Peters, P. (1989) *Thriving on Chaos: Handbook for a Management Revolution*, London: Macmillan.

Phillips, R. (1995) 'Growth and Diversity: A New Era in Colleges and Universities', in Slowey, M. (ed), *Implementing Change From Within Universities and Colleges: 10 Personal Accounts*, London: Kogan Page.

Powell, F. (1999) 'Adult Education, Cultural Empowerment and Social Equality: The Cork Northside Education Initiative', *Widening Participation and Lifelong Learning: The Journal of the Institute for Access Studies and The European Access Network*, (1) 1, April, 20–27.

Poxton, R. (1996) *Joint Approaches for a Better Old Age. Developing Services through Joint Commissioning*, London: Kings Fund.

Pratt, J., Gordon, P. and Plamping, D. (2000) *Working Whole Systems: Putting Theory into Practice in Organisations*, London: Kings Fund.

Preece, J. (1999) *Combating Social Exclusion in University Adult Education*, Aldershot: Ashgate.

Preece, J., Weatherald, C. and Woodrow, M. (eds) (1998) *Beyond the Boundaries: Exploring the Potential of Widening Provision in Higher Education*, Leicester: NIACE.

Pritchard, C. (2000) *Making Managers in Universities and Colleges*, Buckingham: SRHE.

Quinn, K. (2001) 'Linking Higher Education to the Social Inclusion Agenda: The South East Scotland Wider Access Regional Forum', *Update of Inclusion*, 3, Spring, 14.

Ramsden, B. (2001) *Patterns of Higher Education Institutions in the UK. A Report to the Longer Term Strategy Group of Universities UK*, London: UUK/SCOP.

Rawson, D. (1994) 'Models of Interprofessional Work: Likely Theories and Possibilities', in Leathard, A. (ed), *Going Inter-professional: Working Together for Health and Welfare*, London: Routledge.

Reynolds, S. (1995) 'Amman Valley Enterprise: A Case Study of Adult Education and Community Renewal', in Mayo, M. and Thompson, J. (eds), *Adult Learning: Critical Intelligence and Social Change*, Leicester: NIACE.

Robbins, Lord L. C. (1963) *Higher Education – Report to the Advisory Council for Education*, London: The Stationery Office.

Rubenson, K. (1999) 'Adult Education and Training: The Poor Cousin. An Analysis of OECD Reviews of National Policies for Education', *Scottish Journal of Adult and Continuing Education*, (5) 2, 5–33.

Sargant, N. with Field, J., Francis, H., Schuller, T. and Tuckett, A. (1997) *The Learning Divide A Study of Participation in Adult Learning in the United Kingdom*, Leicester: NIACE.

Schuller, T. and Field, J. (1998) 'Social Capital, Human Capital and the Learning Society', *International Journal of Lifelong Education*, (17) 4, 226–35.

Schuller, T., Raffe, D., Morgan-Klein, B. and Clarke, I. (1999) *Part-Time Higher Education: Policy, Practice and Experience*, London: Jessica Kingsley.

Searle-Chatterjee, M. (1999) 'Life Histories and How they Shape Our-selves/behavior: Occupation, Biography and New Social Movements', *The Sociological Review*, (47) 2, May, 258–79.

Slowey, M. (ed) (1995) *Implementing Change From Within Universities and Colleges: 10 Personal Accounts*, London: Kogan Page.

Smale, G. (1996) *Mapping Change and Innovation*, London: The Stationery Office.

Stacey, R. (2001) 'Managing Change in a World of Diversity', *Developing People*, Summer, 4–5.

Stanley, L. (1998) 'The Reports: Two Feminist Views on Educational Policy-making and Politics. From Papers Getting a Good Report? Gendering Dearing, Feminising Kennedy', paper for the conference on Gender in Further and Higher Education in the New Era: Manchester.

Stock, A. (1996) 'Lifelong Learning: Thirty Years of Educational Change', in Raggatt, P., Edwards, R. and Small, N. (eds), *The Learning Society*, London: Routledge.

Storan, J. (2001) 'Thinking Strategically About Widening Participation: Reviewing HEI's Initial Strategic Statements', *Update of Inclusion*, 3, Spring, 2–5.

Stuart, M. and Thomson, A. (1995) *Engaging With Difference: The Other in Adult Education*, Leicester: NIACE.

Tallantyre, F. (1995) 'Using Projects for Dynamic Intervention in the Curriculum of Higher Education', in Slowey, M. (ed), *Implementing Change From Within Universities and Colleges: 10 Personal Accounts*, London: Kogan Page.

Tanner, R. (1990) *Managing on the Edge, How Successful Companies use Conflict to Stay Ahead*, Harmondsworth: Penguin.

Taylor, R. (1995) 'Accessibility and Institutional Change', in Slowey, M. (ed), *Implementing Change From Within Universities and Colleges: 10 Personal Accounts*, London: Kogan Page.

Thompson, J. (1980) *Adult Education for a Change*, London: Hutchinson.

Thompson, J. (1983) *Learning Liberation: Women's Response to Men's Education*, London: Croom Helm.

Thompson, J. (1995) 'Feminism and Women's Education', in Mayo, M. and Thompson, J. (eds), *Adult Learning Critical Intelligence and Social Change*, Leicester: NIACE.

Thompson, J. (2000) *Stretching the Academy: The Politics and Practice of Widening Participation in Higher Education*, Leicester: NIACE.

Thomson, A. (2001) 'Student Cash in Melting Pot', *The Times Higher Education Supplement*, 5 October.

Tight, M. (1998) 'Bridging the Learning Divide: The Nature of Politics of Participation', *Studies in the Education of Adults*, (30) 2, October, 110–19.

Tobias, R. (1998) 'Who Needs Education and Training? The Learning Experiences and Perspectives of Adults from Working Class Backgrounds', *Studies in the Education of Adults*, (30) 2, October, 120–41.

Tomlinson, J. (1996) *Inclusive Learning: Report of The Learning Difficulties and Disabilities Committee*, Coventry: FEFC.

Trotman, C. and Lewis, A. (1990) *Education and Training: The Experience and Needs of Miners Redundant from Cynheidre and Betws Collieries in South Wales*, Swansea: Valleys Initiative for Adult Education.

Tuckett, A. and Sargant, N. (1999) *Marking Time: The NIACE Survey on Adult Participation in Learning*, Leicester: NIACE.

United Nations Educational, Scientific and Cultural Organisation (UNESCO) (1996) *Learning, The Treasure Within* (TheDelors Report), Paris: UNESCO,

Usher, R., Bryant, I. and Johnston, R. (1997) *Adult Education and the Postmodern Challenge: Learning Beyond the Limits*, London: Routledge.

Utley, A. (2001) 'Access Plan that Totally Backfired', *The Times Higher Education Supplement*, 6 September.

Walmsley, J. (1993) *Working Together for Change: Equal People*, workbook three, Buckingham: Open University Press.

Ward, K. and Taylor, R. (1986) *Adult Education and the Working Class: Education for the Missing Millions*, London: Croom Helm.

Watson, D. and Taylor, R. (1998) *Lifelong Learning and the University: A Post Dearing Agenda*, London: Falmer Press.

Westwood, S. (1992) 'When Class became Community', in Rattansi, A. and Reeder, D. (eds), *Rethinking Radical Education*, London: Lawerence and Wishart.

Wicks, M. (2000) Keynote Address to Universities Association of Continuing Education Conference, April 2000.

Wistow, G. (1994) 'Community Care Futures. Inter-agency relationships – Stability or Continuing Change?', in Titterton, M. (ed), *Caring for People in the Community: The New Welfare*, London: Jessica Kingsley.

Woodrow, M. (2001) 'Politics not Paper. Why Monitoring Matters for Widening Participation Projects', *Update on Inclusion: Widening Participation in Higher Education*, 3, Spring, 8–10.

Zera, A. and Jupp, T. (1998) 'If at First You Don't Succeed, Don't Bother. What Has to be Done to Widen Participation in Further Education?', internal research paper, Tower Hamlets College.

Index

Other titles from NIACE

Stretching the academy: The politics and practice of widening participation in higher education

Edited by Jane Thompson

ISBN 1 86201 091 9, 2000, 192pp, £15.95

A major new intervention in the widening participation debate by academics active in radical politics. This collection of essays brings together critical analyses and inspirational prose, rooted in the authority of experience and practice. Essential reading for all those concerned with the part played by Higher Education in widening participation.

'An important and appropriately theorised re-assertion of the values, knowledge, contexts and methods of social purpose adult education and their potential interface with HE'

(Adults Learning, February 2001)

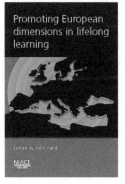

Promoting European dimensions in lifelong learning

Edited by John Field

ISBN 1 86201 048 X, 2001, 200pp, £15.95

This collection seeks to learn the lessons of experiences of building a European dimension to lifelong learning. It includes analysis of EU education and training; accounts by managers and practitioners of European projects, ESF programmes and transnational projects; a series of 'how-to' chapters covering topics such as 'how to write a successful proposal'; and a guide to resources and information sources. This is a work of reference for the busy professional and a source of know-how for managers and others involved in developing the European dimension of adult learning.

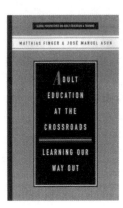

Adult education at the crossroads: Learning our way out

Matthias Finger and José Manuel Asún

ISBN 1 86201 108 7, 2001, 228pp, £15.95

An assessment of where adult education now stands – the traditions out of which it came, its current problems, and possible futures. By surveying the ideas of seminal adult education thinkers as they developed historically in Europe, North America and later the Third World, the authors show how today's very different context has eroded that original vision and purpose.

"More than a text; it is a 'must read' for any serious adult educator"
(Phyllis Cunningham, Northern Illinois University)

Inviting learning: An exhibition of risk and enrichment in adult education practice

Peter Willis

ISBN 1 86201 129 X, 2002, 244pp, hardback, £39.95

Using an emerging approach, this fascinating text presents adult education practice as a 'lived' experience using expressive research method to portray rather than explain or analyse. Willis explores different episodes of adult education practice, explains the expressive method used and looks at their significance for practice.

Understanding motivation for lifelong learning

Jim Smith and Andrea Spurling
Co-published with the Campaign for Learning

ISBN 1 90310 700 8, 2001, 130pp, £14.95

Understanding the motivation to learn is increasingly recognised by policy makers and practitioners as the key to the creation of the Learning Age. However, despite many years of research in a number of fields, no comprehensive assessment of motivation for lifelong learning has existed until now. In addition to offering an impressive synthesis and development of existing research, this book maps the factors influencing motivation across the three spheres of workplace, home and community and also explores the practical implications of an understanding of motivation for policy. Required reading for all those involved in creating the learning age.

Online learning and social exclusion

Alan Clarke

ISBN 1 86201 115 X, 2002, 96pp, £15.95

Online learning has the potential to overcome the barriers of pace, place and time of learning so that it can in principle deliver learning to almost any location with a telephone line. This book considers the nature of the different approaches to online learning in relation to adults who are socially or economically disadvantaged to reveal how this potential can be realised.

These books are available from:
Publications Sales
NIACE
21 De Montfort Street
Leicester, LE1 7GE
or order online at:
www.niace.org.uk/publications